Workbook

Irene Barrall
Lizzie Wright

B2+

Business Partner

Contents

1 ▶ Market research

Terms in market research

1 Choose the correct option in italics to complete the excerpt from a report.

> We carried out primary [1]*research / market / promotion* on our [2]*target / objective / goal* audience and now plan to arrange further feedback. The next stage will use a combination of both online [3]*assessments / surveys / evaluations* and focus [4]*panels / teams / groups*. In order to carry this out as cost effectively as possible, the sample [5]*amount / quantity / size* will be small. In addition, [6]*primary / secondary / minor* research will also be carried out using existing data available on the internet.

2 Complete the meeting notes with the words in the box. There is one extra word.

> analysis   customer satisfaction   in-depth   qualitative
> quantitative   researchers   respondents   tester

Action points

- Select a product [1]_____ group to use the updated app and report back on new features.
- Contact any [2]_____ who have not yet returned their surveys from batch 1. Check whether they need any assistance in answering questions.
- Create a batch [3]_____ questionnaire to identify whether there was a positive reaction to the new app from the target audience.
- Brief the [4]_____ about the level of detail required when questions are answered in the [5]_____ interviews.
- Arrange a meeting to discuss the findings from the data [6]_____ and agree the best method of communicating the information.
- Add details to the report explaining why [7]_____ research methods are being used in the second part of the study (as the client wishes to use statistics).

3 Complete the words for these definitions.

1 Another term for secondary research: d _ _ _ research

2 To measure or assess how people feel about a product: g _ _ _ _ _

3 The effect that something is likely to have: i _ _ _ _ _ _

4 To collect data or information from a range of sources: g _ _ _ _ _ _

5 To introduce a new product into the market: l _ _ _ _ _ _

6 Describing a realistic plan that has a chance of succeeding: v _ _ _ _ _ _

Grammar Question tags

1 Match the statements (1–6) with the question tags (a–f).

1 The focus group meeting is this afternoon,

2 These statistics are reliable,

3 No one has seen this report,

4 The market research questionnaire isn't ready yet,

5 Nobody is using this computer at the moment,

6 The survey questions weren't too difficult,

a aren't they?

b are they?

c isn't it?

d were they?

e have they?

f is it?

2 Complete the sentences with the question tags in the box.

| aren't they   do they   doesn't it   shall we   will we   won't they |

1 Let's consider all the facts before we make a decision, _____ ?

2 Everyone in conference room three is here for the focus group meeting, _____ ?

3 Honestly, nobody believes these statistics, _____ ?

4 The participants will be here by 10 o'clock, _____ ?

5 This data helps us to plan our marketing strategy, _____ ?

6 I think you and I won't have enough time to attend the marketing meeting, _____ ?

3 Complete the dialogue with one word in each gap.

A: So, the aim of this focus group ¹_____ to select a group of participants that represent our target consumers, isn't ²_____ ?

B: That's correct, but none of your team has got experience in organising this type of group, ³_____ they?

A: Well, Martina worked in Marketing in her previous role, ⁴_____ she?

B: Yes, and Karl ⁵_____ excellent organisational skills, doesn't he? Perhaps they could work together?

A: I'm not sure. It's a big responsibility, ⁶_____ ⁷_____ ? Neither Karl nor Martina have a good knowledge of our target consumers. After all, they only joined the company six months ago, ⁸_____ they?

B: Well, why don't we get another couple of people with consumer experience to join the team? For example, Julia and Chris ⁹_____ working on a project at the moment, are ¹⁰_____ ?

A: No, but they won't want to work on the focus group, ¹¹_____ they? They both made it clear in the meeting last week that they didn't want to be involved.

B: Well, they might not have a choice. Look, let's leave it there, ¹²_____ we? We can talk again on Monday and make a decision.

Reading

Focus groups: FAQs

1 _____

In business contexts, it can often be useful to gather opinions on a product or service during the development stage. For instance, in a focus group, participants might describe what they like or dislike about a company's product or those of its competitors. Based on information gained from the group discussion, modifications or changes could then be made. Later in the process, focus group opinions may be used to gather feedback on a proposed advertising or marketing campaign.

2 _____

Focus groups are most useful for qualitative rather than quantitative research. Quantitative research (which includes surveys, questionnaires and polls) relies on gathering measurable data which is often transformed into statistics. In contrast, qualitative research aims to understand the reasons and background for opinions. Focus groups and interviews allow participants to explain and expand on their opinions in relation to a topic, product or brand.

3 _____

The context is important when deciding how large or small to make a focus group. Most market research companies will have groups of ten to twelve participants. However, some research can work better with smaller groups of around five to seven people.

4 _____

Although many businesses may prefer participants to meet face-to-face, it is also possible to arrange focus groups via video conferencing or online. Ideally the environment should be relaxed and comfortable.

5 _____

The group usually includes a moderator whose role is to put forward the questions or topics for discussion. Although the moderator may guide the discussion by managing timekeeping, keeping the group on topic and summarising key points at the end, their main role is to remain neutral and encourage participants to contribute. To facilitate this, the moderator should have excellent listening skills and use body language and eye contact to show interest in what the focus group has to say.

6 _____

Some experts express concerns about the reliability of research gained from focus groups. The small number of people in a group means that the information gained is often specific and may not always be suitable for generalised contexts. Added to this is whether the opinions of participants are reliable, or if they are saying what they think the moderator wants to hear. Some groups might also contain people who dominate or influence the opinions of other participants. Moreover, it can be difficult to analyse the data. However, it can be a more cost-effective method of gathering data compared with interviewing people individually. An effective moderator can also gain insights from participants' body language and their level of interaction. The findings can produce data that is easier to communicate than complex statistics and the flexibility of focus groups means that they can be used for a wide range of topics.

---

1 Read the article and label the paragraphs (1–6) with the correct heading (a–f).

a Are they used for particular research?   **d** Why use focus groups?

b What are the pros and cons?   **e** How many participants are required?

c How is the research carried out?   **f** How is the group run?

2 Read the article again. Decide if these statements are *true* (T), *false* (F) or the information is *not given* (NG).

1 Participants are usually given the opportunity to try the product.   ___

2 The qualitative method is most useful for data to be expressed in numeric form.   ___

3 The moderator should avoid putting forward their own point of view.   ___

4 Moderators use both verbal and non-verbal strategies to put people at ease.   ___

5 There are concerns regarding the dependability of data from focus groups.   ___

6 A disadvantage of focus groups is that they can only be used for limited subjects.   ___

3 Tick (✓) the two statements which are supported by the article.

1 Focus groups can be used to gain insights into opinions and also gather feedback.   ☐

2 A disadvantage of focus groups is that discussions need to be carried out in person.   ☐

3 Data gained from focus groups is regarded as more trustworthy than other methods.   ☐

4 Participants in focus groups are given the opportunity to describe their views in detail.   ☐

Functional language

Using leading and open questions to effect

1 Choose the correct option to complete the questions.

1 What are your thoughts ___ doing an online training course?

   a on   **b** in   **c** around

2 What do you think ___ working longer hours on Monday and Wednesday?

   a by   **b** on   **c** about

3 Would your team ___ learning new sales strategies?

   a have interest in   **b** be interesting for   **c** be interested in

4 Has your intern ___ speaking to HR to discuss options?

   a concluded   **b** considered   **c** contracted

5 Have you thought ___ offering the guests refreshments when they arrive?

   a about   **b** on   **c** around

6 How would the department ___ about working in smaller teams?

   a think   **b** conclude   **c** feel

7 How ___ up the primary research with a focus group?

   a about following   **b** don't we follow   **c** do we follow

Responding to questions during a presentation

2 Match 1–6 with a–f to complete the sentences and questions.

1 To be perfectly frank,		**a**	in Human Resources to answer that.
2 Can you clarify what you mean		**b**	What's the question exactly?
3 Can we discuss this one-to-one		**c**	I can't give you those figures yet.
4 I'm sorry, I didn't understand that.		**d**	that many people feel strongly about this.
5 Let me put you in touch with someone		**e**	by 'streamline resources'?
6 We need to be mindful		**f**	after the team meeting tomorrow?

3 Put the words in italics in the correct order to make responses to questions.

1 Sorry, we can't *very well / because the / is bad / hear you / connection*

_____

2 It's a bad line *just repeat / so let me / to be sure / I understood / your question*

_____

3 If you can *directly / email me / that question, / I'll respond / to you*

_____

4 This is a very *delicate topic / to / respond / sensitively / need to / which we*

_____

5 I'm afraid that *outside / presentation / question is / the scope / of today's*

_____

6 Sorry, can I *for / just / pushed / stop you / there as / time / we are*

_____

Writing Reports – Summary findings

1 Choose the correct option in italics to complete the summary of a market research report.

Summary findings: Customer survey regarding Chocomax, our new chocolate bar

A recent customer survey [1]*demonstrated / arranged / believed* that many of the changes proposed for our confectionary range are regarded as positive. The survey asked 500 people to comment on the new packaging. Over [2]*double / twice / half* of those surveyed approved of the colour and design. Most [3]*answers / reactions / respondents* felt that the image is still instantly recognisable. [4]*Over to / More than / Above which* three quarters believed that it gave our product range a fresh, modern look and [5]*just / almost / near* over a quarter agreed that it made our products stand out from our competitors. The [6]*main / mass / majority* of our customers were also in agreement that our commitment to using 100 percent recyclable materials was welcomed, although 15 percent of the 500 [7]*public / participants / members* commented that the new material did not match the luxury branding of the product. Nevertheless, [8]*few / none / several* of the data suggested that the new design or material would make customers less likely to buy the chocolate bars. In summary, the survey [9]*confirmed / completed / demanded* that we should continue to move forward with our plans. However, [10]*these final / a result / the findings* also highlighted some concerns about the quality of the product. We are carrying out some additional market research on this issue.

---

2 Match the phrases in the box (a–g) with the survey findings (1–7).

Comments Topic: new version of Chocomax chocolate bar	% of respondents (500 people in survey)	
1 Think the new recipe uses cheaper ingredients.	47%	☐
2 Would pay more for a better quality product.	33%	☐
3 Prefer the flavour of the new recipe compared to the original.	1%	☐
4 Think the original product was bigger and tasted better.	95%	☐
5 Are unlikely to buy this bar if the price increases.	68%	☐
6 Say the quality of the product does not reflect the luxury brand image.	75%	☐
7 Would like to see more flavours introduced to the range.	25%	☐

a The majority	of the	participants respondents responses target audience	think / feel that … believe that … confirm that … indicate that …
b Almost none			
c Three quarters			
d Around a third			
e Just under half	of those	surveyed	are in agreement that … raise concerns that … prefer …
f A quarter			
g More than two thirds			

3 Write a report summary of about 225 words. Include the following:

- information from the survey in Exercise 2.

- functional language from Exercise 2 on page 16 of the coursebook.

4 Choose the sentence which best describes what the reader is likely to infer from your summary.

a There are some issues with quality control but they are unlikely to affect sales.

b The changes to the recipe have not proved popular and require further thought.

c An increase in price is inevitable because the cost of ingredients will rise.

2 Give and take

Vocabulary Giving back

1 Put the letters in brackets in the correct order to complete the information.

How to develop collaboration in your team

Create a(n) ¹_____ environment that helps staff to develop. (n g r t n u u r i)

Organise group activities so that no one feels ²_____ or alone in the team. (e i o l a d s t)

Encourage ³_____ so that new employees can learn from those with more experience. (i m g n t e o r n)

Build trust by being honest, open and ⁴_____ in your communication style. (n d d c a i)

Arrange regular meetings where team members can give ⁵_____ to their ⁶_____ . (k e b f e c d a) (s e p e r)

Discuss the ⁷_____ of collaboration. Explain how it will help projects. (e b e s t n f i)

Lead the way with a management style that is ⁸_____ and shows you care about your team. (p o o i a t s s c m a n e)

2 Complete the sentences with the words in the box.

| beneficial   call   cooperative   heart   inclusion   interests   shots   two-way |

1 The success of the project was due to the _____ atmosphere between departments.

2 Effective communication means that listening needs to be a(n) _____ street.

3 Mentoring can be mutually _____ for both management and staff.

4 The board of directors had the companies best _____ at _____ when making these changes.

5 This role requires a manager who prefers to work collaboratively rather than _____ the _____ .

6 What steps has your organisation taken to improve _____ in the decision-making process?

Grammar Cleft sentences

1 Choose the correct option to complete the sentences.

1 Look, it is the Project Manager who is requesting these amendments, ___ .

   a isn't the clients   **b** not the clients   **c** none of the clients

2 ___ before we leave for Gdansk, is check that all the documents are correct.

   a What will we do   **b** We will do what   **c** What we will do

3 It is the board of directors ___ the final decision on this matter.

   a who are making   **b** what have made   **c** they make

4 ___ to do was check the data before putting it on the website.

   a Something they fail   **b** Which they have failed   **c** The thing they failed

5 The thing I like most about this candidate ___ so enthusiastic about the products.

   a which is she is   **b** is that she is   **c** that she is

6 The finance director ___ you need to discuss these budget issues with, not me.

   a is the person   **b** the person who   **c** who the person is

2 Choose the two correct options in italics to complete each sentence.

1 *The thing / Something / Which* we must do is make sure the contract is signed.

2 Thankfully, it *was / will be / is* the HR manager who has to make this difficult decision.

3 Of course, *what / it / something* we need to consider is the time that this will take.

4 *The thing / What / That* staff like about this company is that they are treated fairly.

5 It *won't / was / wasn't* an issue with quality control which caused these delays.

6 *Something / Things / The things* they focused on were health risks and lack of funds.

3 Put the words in the correct order to make cleft sentences.

1 compromise on / and reliability / are quality / that we cannot / the things

_____

2 from home / allow employees / did was to / successful business / to work / what one

_____

3 are finance / that most interest / or consultancy / the areas of business / graduates

_____

4 make sure that / completed before / do is / the deadline / the work is / what I will

_____

5 cause of / it was a / not our staff / technological problem / that was the / the delay,

_____

6 is having regular / meetings to / something that / update the team / works for us

_____

Listening 1 🔊 2.01 **Match the terms (1–5) with the definitions (a–g). There are two extra definitions. Then listen to an interview with an HR expert about the importance of empathy in the workplace and check your answers.**

1	emotional intelligence	**a**	showing feelings of annoyance or anger
2	communication breakdown	**b**	when people stop talking, listening and exchanging information effectively
3	sympathy	**c**	understanding what someone is feeling or experiencing
4	empathy	**d**	pity or compassion for another person
5	make hard calls	**e**	take difficult decisions or actions
		f	explain a problem in a calm and relaxed manner
		g	an understanding of your own feelings and also those of others

2 **Complete the summary of the podcast with one word in each gap. Then listen again and check your answers.**

Empathy in the workplace – an interview with Mia Newton, HR Director and Trainer

In today's interview, Mia Newton discusses the importance of
1_____ intelligence in the 2_____ for both
3_____ and employees. Some of the issues that Mia will look
at include the importance of expressing feelings 4_____ in
the work environment and their role in creating positive interpersonal
5_____ . She will help listeners understand key terms such
as *sympathy* and 6_____ and also give practical examples of
what can happen when communication fails. Her main message is that
7_____ and 8_____ emotions are key skills for anyone
working with people in a supervisory role and should be an essential part
of every manager's tool kit.

3 **Read the statements about the management problem Mia describes in the podcast. Decide if they are *true* (T) or *false* (F).**

1 The manager believed that the employee returning to work would be able to carry out her normal workload. ___

2 The thing the manager failed to do was check that he had interpreted the situation correctly. ___

3 The employee initially felt positive and enthusiastic about her return to work. ___

4 One issue was that the returning employee's colleague was unable to do the extra work. ___

Functional language

Renegotiation of an agreement

1 Complete the dialogue with the phrases (a–f) in the box.

a discuss this face-to-face	**c** best interests in mind	**e** be perfectly frank
b after careful consideration	**d** having had a chance to	**f** drawing on experience

E: Thanks for coming in today, David. From your email, I had the impression that there might be some issues with our initial agreement.

D: That's right, Emma. To [1]___ , the project is more complicated than we first thought.

E: What makes you think that?

D: Well, [2]___ look through all of the material carefully, it appears that it will require specialised software.

E: Why didn't you mention this in your email?

D: The main reason is that I wanted to [3]___ , so that we can agree how to proceed.

E: OK, but do you think this specialised software will increase costs significantly?

D: Well, no, I don't believe it will. [4]___ , we've written this type of software many times before and the cost would only take us a little above the terms we agreed.

E: What about deadlines? Would it create any problems in terms of delivery date?

D: I've looked at the schedule and, [5]___ , I've worked out how we could do this with only five extra days.

E: Oh, that's actually not as bad as I thought it would be. I wouldn't have a problem changing the agreement along those lines.

D: That's good to hear. Thanks for your understanding. We always approach projects by keeping the client's [6]___ and this solution should provide a much better outcome.

Promoting collaboration

2 Choose the correct option in italics to complete the sentences.

1 Let's be *open / over* today and come *out / up* with some new ideas.

2 So, let me just *check / approve* that we're all on the same *page / book*.

3 I think *each / both* perspectives are valid because they consider key *issues / views*.

4 I'll come back *at / to* you in a *second / time*, if I may.

5 Any thoughts on how *well / best* to *tackle / hold* this?

6 Roland, what might be the *wins / benefits* of Anya's way of *thoughts / thinking*?

3 Choose the best response to match the function in brackets.

1 There's no way this suggestion would work. (manage different views positively)

    a You never look on the positive side.

    b Let's not dismiss this idea too quickly.

    c Doesn't anyone have a more practical solution?

2 There are many reasons why this is our best option. (quieten louder individuals)

    a Let's consider the options and then move on to the next agenda point.

    b Could you be quiet for a while because nobody else is able to contribute.

    c If I can just stop you there, Jay, because it would be useful to hear other views.

3 We should change to a more local venue. (make people engage with others' ideas)

    a Perhaps you can suggest a more sensible idea, Mina?

    b Mina, any reflections on Toby's suggestion?

    c That won't work, Toby. Mina, any thoughts?

Writing   Emails – Stating requirements

1 **Proofread and correct the first draft of an email. There are ten missing words. Hint: look for missing articles, pronouns, prepositions, etc.**

Dear Michael,

As we discussed in our meeting today, here is a summary of the main areas where we require improvements in team performance for next project.

Firstly, we like you to schedule weekly project updates. As project leader, you need
5   check progress and communicate any concerns to your manager that problems can be solved quickly and efficiently.

Secondly, it is important that you arrange face-to-face meetings with the client the start of the project to discuss requirements. It is also necessary to arrange regular calls to out if they require changes to the brief. We expect you to inform the team
10   of any amendments immediately.

Next, could you arrange for a member of your team to prepare online survey after each project is complete order to check customer satisfaction. Arrange follow calls for customers who do not respond to the survey. Please summarise the findings in a brief report for your overview meeting with the department director.

15   Finally, we realise that you have taken on additional responsibility in your new role and we would therefore like to offer you the opportunity to have further training in project organisation. Speak to the HR Manager next week more information on course dates.

Kind regards,

20   Bente

2 **Write an email of about 225 words to a trainee stating some requirements for the next part of the course. Include the following:**

- notes from the meeting.
- longer phrases and more formal language.

Notes from meeting:
Completed first part of the course and passed exam.

Requirements for next part of course:
- attend seminars/lectures more regularly
- more preparation needed for projects
- hand assignments in on time
- meet tutor weekly to discuss progress

3 **What is the main purpose of your email?**

a To identify and give reasons for goals and explain what will happen if they are not met.

b To explain the impact of the trainee's behaviour on their chances of passing the course.

c To inform the trainee of how to improve performance and specific actions required.

3 > Money matters

Vocabulary

Word building – verbs, adjectives and nouns

1 Complete the sentences with the correct form of the words in brackets.

1 If the money is _____ from the account within thirty days, no interest will be paid. (withdraw)

2 Investors should discuss _____ decisions with an advisor before buying shares. (finance)

3 The fees on the business account were _____ , which is why they changed banks. (prohibit)

4 He has always been good with figures, which is why he chose a career in _____ . (bank)

5 There was a problem with the money _____ that we actioned last week so we've contacted the supplier. (transfer)

6 Please remember to include the name of the _____ on the bank forms. (pay)

7 She wants to gain experience in _____ , so she's working as an intern with one of the largest firms in the city. (account)

8 Mobile banking allows me to make _____ into my account without going into a branch. (deposit)

Personal banking

2 Use the clues to complete the word grid.

1 money that you pay to a professional person or company for their work

2 a written statement showing how much money you owe someone for goods or services you have received

3 a printed official document that you buy in a bank and send to someone so that they can exchange it for money in a bank (two words)

4 a plastic card with your signature that you can use to pay for things (two words)

5 an amount of money that you pay regularly for using an office, etc. that belongs to someone else

6 an instruction given to a bank to regularly pay money out of an account to a person or organisation (two words)

7 a printed piece of paper that can be used instead of money to pay for things

8 money that you have put in a bank to be used later rather than spent straight away

Grammar Phrasal verbs

1 **Choose the correct option in italics to complete the sentences.**

1 Some members of staff are finding it difficult to get *through / by / in* on their salary.

2 When taking *out / in / off* a mortgage, clients need to consider interest rates.

3 You should put some money *by / in / on* every month for unexpected expenses.

4 Have you set a separate account *on / in / up* to pay for bills and rent?

5 If you fall behind *to / with / off* your payments, there will be a penalty charge.

6 The team is looking *onward / about / forward* to finishing the project.

2 **Tick (✓) the correct sentence (a or b). Sometimes both sentences are correct.**

1 **a** We would save money if we didn't eat out so often. ☐

   b We would save money if we didn't eat so often out. ☐

2 **a** The company needs to pay the loan back before September. ☐

   b The company needs to pay back the loan before September. ☐

3 **a** Many of their clients have run large debts up through overspending. ☐

   b Many of their clients have run up large debts through overspending. ☐

4 **a** The Finance Manager advised him to cut his expenses down on. ☐

   b The Finance Manager advised him to cut down on his expenses. ☐

5 **a** Too many people put speaking to an advisor about important financial decisions off. ☐

   b Too many people put off speaking to an advisor about important financial decisions. ☐

6 **a** They will carry on paying back the loan with the current terms and conditions. ☐

   b They will carry paying back the loan on with the current terms and conditions. ☐

3 **Match the correct sentence (1–6) in Exercise 2 with the type of phrasal verb (a–c).**

a Transitive, separable   ___ , ___

b Intransitive, i.e. no object   ___

c Transitive, non-separable   ___ , ___ , ___

Reading

FT

Women want face-to-face financial advice – men just hate the cost

Men and women take very different approaches towards managing their investments, a new study has claimed, with women more likely to opt for face-to-face advice, even though financial advisers can fall short of their expectations.

¹___ , compared with 28 percent of men, according to a new study by EY, the accountancy firm. While men cited high fees for financial advice as their top complaint, women were more concerned about an adviser's lack of knowledge.

Women were also less likely to engage with their financial life as frequently as their male counterparts, with ²___ , compared with almost half of men.

While technology and the ability to review investments online is making decision-making less time-consuming, just 53 percent of women said they check their investments online, ³___ .

'Women view achieving their personal goals as more important than investment performance, so a deep understanding by the advisers of the personal goals and priorities is vital to satisfying female clients,' said Gill Lofts, head of Wealth & Asset Management at EY.

Drawing on the findings of the study, ⁴ ___ , she said women placed particular value on advisers who can clearly explain their investment views and decisions.

'We believe women are looking for a financial coach who will work with them on their personal goals throughout their life events, in a much more collaborative and consultative fashion than they're currently experiencing,' she added.

Ms Lofts cited a separate study by the Centre for Talent Innovation, ⁵___ . 'Women will use tech, but when it comes to more complex decision-making processes, they expect face-to-face meetings to be high quality.'

The findings build on existing research on the gender investment gap, such as the commonly held view that ⁶___ than men. Ms Lofts said that when investment decisions become more complex, 'one gets the feeling that women want to go into more detail and want to understand fully how things are operating'.

⁷___ , she emphasised the importance for wealth managers to 'actively attract and retain what is an increasingly important client segment'.

---

1 **Read and complete the article with the extracts (a–h). One extract is not used.**

a which was based on interviews with 250 wealthy investors

b only 27 percent of women stating that they reviewed their investments weekly or daily

c The survey revealed that women were more likely to regularly check their portfolio

d which found that 73 percent of women felt their financial adviser misunderstood them

e Regarding the future of female investing

f as opposed to 68 percent of men

g Just under half of female investors said they preferred to see an adviser in person

h women are more risk-averse investors

2 **Decide if these statements describe *male* (M) or *female* (F) investors.**

1 The cost of financial advice was one of the main issues. ___

2 They weren't always convinced by the advisor's expertise. ___

3 They're more likely to review their investments on a regular basis. ___

4 A higher percentage used technology to check investments. ___

5 They appreciate detailed explanations when discussing investments. ___

6 They want a lot of background information to have a clear understanding. ___

3 **Tick (✓) the statements which are more likely to have been made by a woman according to the article.**

1 I'm happy to discuss this online, but I'd prefer it if we could meet to go over the details. ☐

2 The main reason that I changed my financial advisor is that he charged too much. ☐

3 This app is useful for checking how my shares are doing, but I spend far too much time on it. ☐

4 Can you talk me through the performance figures to explain why you think this is such a good investment? ☐

Functional language

Fact-based and emotion-based presentations

1 Match 1–8 with a–h to complete the sentences.

1 I'd like to take this opportunity	**a**	all aware, this is a key market for us.
2 Try and picture the looks on	**b**	breakdown of expenditure for this month?
3 Of course, as you are	**c**	more magical than a candle-lit dining room?
4 Now, turning our attention	**d**	to describe the benefits of our service.
5 Can you give me a brief	**e**	will react when we announce the location.
6 Imagine how everyone	**f**	the anticipation of what is about to happen.
7 Your guest will feel	**g**	to financial matters, here's the price list.
8 Can you think of anything	**h**	visitors' faces as they enter the reception area.

Defending ideas and describing consequences

2 Put the words in brackets in the correct order to complete the introduction to a presentation.

> Hello. For those of you who haven't worked with me on the manufacturing stage of a furniture project before, let me introduce myself. I'm Olga Petrov and I'm the Production Manager. For the next step we are considering using outside contractors for some of the technical aspects of the project. ¹(*warrant / which / these / are / reasons / the*) outsourcing some of the tasks. Firstly, ²(*the / picture / considered / big / when / we*), we could see that our production costs were increasing steadily and it would become more expensive to continue doing this work in-house. Also, our technical requirements would have become more complicated. So, if we don't outsource, then we will need to modernise our resources. ³(*fail / to / if / act, / we / then*) the increased production costs are likely to result in raised prices for our customers. ⁴(*the / of / that / would / consequence / be*) we lose out to our competitors who are producing cheaper products. Naturally, we ⁵(*might / see / objections / there / can / be / why*). Colleagues have raised concerns about quality control if we choose to outsource and, trust me, we have taken this into consideration. However, I am certain that ⁶(*best / opportunity / is / this / the / idea*) we have of remaining competitive in a shrinking market.

1 _____ 4 _____

2 _____ 5 _____

3 _____ 6 _____

3 Complete the sentences. Then decide if the sentences are *Defending ideas* (D) or *Talking about consequences* (C).

1 Committing to this a_ _ _ _ _ would m_ _ _ _ that we would need to retrain staff. ____

2 Let me b_ _ _ _ _ d _ _ _ _ the main r_ _ _ _ _ _ _ why this is our best way forward. ____

3 This i_ _ _ _ is the best o_ _ _ _ _ _ _ _ _ _ _ we have of increasing market share. ____

4 We s_ _ _ _ _ _ rethink our c_ _ _ _ _ _ _ strategy as otherwise our profits will likely suffer next quarter. ____

5 We won't a_ _ _ _ _ _ _ our collective t_ _ _ _ _ if we don't agree on a common approach. ____

6 I'm pleased to confirm that we have the b_ _ _ _ _ _ _ of o_ _ _ _ _ on the board. ____

Writing   Letter of complaint

1 **Read the letter of complaint. Replace the underlined phrases (1–8) with the more formal phrases in the box (a–h).**

a	Unless you do this, we shall be forced to	**e**	anticipate any issues
b	dealt with this matter most unprofessionally	**f**	gave notice that
c	express our dissatisfaction with	**g**	your prompt response
d	have damaged our trust in your company	**h**	request that you kindly

Dear Sir/Madam,

I am writing to ¹complain about ___ your service. Three months ago, my company contacted your hotel to book rooms and facilities for two training courses. The first training course took place this week and the second is scheduled for next month. We reserved thirty rooms in your hotel and also a large conference room. We ²told you ___ we required single rooms and breakfast for all participants. We also requested tea and coffee facilities in the conference room and audiovisual equipment for presentations. Due to the block booking of rooms and meals, we also agreed on a 10 percent discount.

Having informed you well in advance of our requirements and receiving written confirmation that everything was in order, we did not ³expect any problems ___ . However, on arrival at the hotel, we were told that some of the rooms were shared and that the audiovisual equipment was not available. In addition, participants reported that their breakfast was cold and no tea and coffee was available in the conference room. We spoke to the assistant manager who refused to help. Finally, when we came to pay the bill, the 10 percent discount had not been included. We feel that you have ⁴handled this matter badly ___ and your actions ⁵mean that we now do not have confidence in your hotel ___ .

As a long-standing customer, we ⁶expect you to ___ resolve these matters for our future booking and also increase the discount to 15 percent due to the problems we have experienced. ⁷If you do not sort this matter out, we will ___ find another hotel for the second training course.

We look forward to ⁸hearing from you soon ___ .

Yours faithfully,

Kim Hemingway

Training Coordinator

2 **Read the notes below. Then write a formal letter of complaint to the supplier of about 225 words. Include the following information:**

- State your reason for writing.

- Include details of the problem.

- Say what action you require and include a warning.

- Begin and end the letter appropriately.

- 10 weeks ago: ordered 2,000 key rings printed with company logo (for conference)
  Monday: received letter to say only 75% of order will have logo

- 12% discount negotiated on original order
  Price quoted on letter received from supplier does not include discount

- Called customer services – no response

- Immediate action/resolution + 25% discount. If no action, will find another supplier.

3 **Choose the option which best describes your letter in Exercise 2.**

a Displeased, providing an outline of your opinions and feelings regarding the problem

b Factual and formal, giving examples of issues and stating the action required

c Polite but direct, making strong demands about what you wish to happen

4 > Challenges

Vocabulary **Collocations: the environment**

1 **Complete the words to make collocations.**

1 pose a t__r__ __t

2 extreme w__ __t__ __r

3 high t__ __ p__ __ __t__ __ __s

4 climate c__ __n__e

5 humid a__ __o__ __h__ __e

6 growing d__m__ __d

7 unstable e__v__ __ __ __ __m__ __t

8 face d__f__ __ __ __ __L__ __ __s

2 **Complete the excerpt from an interview using six of the collocations from Exercise 1.**

G: We are speaking to agriculture expert, Richard Hind. Richard, we've recently seen a number of examples of [1]_____ around the globe, such as floods and droughts. Are you concerned that this could [2]_____ to the success of our agricultural crops this year?

R: Yes, I am, Gemma. Both Europe and North America have experienced unusually [3]_____ this summer. For example, this July was the warmest on record for many countries. In addition, areas with a(n) [4]_____ will find growing conditions particularly challenging. This is because although water vapour in the air is good for growth, too much can damage plants.

G: So, do you think that farmers are likely to [5]_____ with their crops this year?

R: Yes, that's certainly a possibility. When conditions suddenly change, it can create a(n) [6]_____ for growing plants. Reports suggest that farms growing cereals or vegetables will be the worst affected.

3 **Complete the sentences with the words in the box.**

embrace   potential   predict   production   protect   sustainable

1 The report shows that coffee _____ is a major source of income in developing countries.

2 We _____ a problem with delivery times due to the issues with the supply chain.

3 As an organisation, we need to _____ the challenge of adopting clean energy and reducing our use of fossil fuels.

4 Some countries have banned the use of harmful pesticides in agriculture in order to _____ the environment.

5 Steps to implementing _____ solutions for cutting waste include setting clear targets and measuring progress towards them.

6 If neither side is able to find areas of agreement, it could result in the _____ failure of these climate talks.

Grammar   Perfect aspect

1 Complete the table with the correct form of the verbs.

Present Perfect	Past Perfect	Future Perfect
has/have become	1 _____	2 _____
3 _____	had used	4 _____
5 _____	6 _____	will have forgotten
has/have lived	7 _____	8 _____

2 Choose the correct response.

1 You mentioned that you're looking forward to this time next year. Why is that?

   a I had finished my exams and gone on holiday.

   b Well, I'll have just finished my final exams.

   c Because I've recently finished some exams.

2 Can you give me an overview of the tasks that have been completed so far?

   a The engineers have just installed the latest media technology in the new smart flat.

   b The engineers had installed the latest media technology in the new smart flat.

   c The engineers will have installed the latest media technology in the new smart flat.

3 What happened just before Carl's accident?

   a He has picked up the package, and then he had slipped on some water.

   b He will have picked up the package, and then he did slip on some water.

   c He had picked up the package, and then he slipped on some water.

4 So, what did you think of the new software when you first saw it?

   a I'll never have seen anything as advanced so it will be amazing.

   b Well, I'd never seen anything as advanced before so I was amazed.

   c I've never seen anything as advanced so I've been amazed.

5 What are the company's goals for the next stage of this research?

   a We've gathered essential data before the experiments are complete.

   b The experiments were complete and we had gathered essential data.

   c By time the experiments are complete, we'll have gathered essential data.

3 Rewrite the forms in bold to correct the mistakes. Three sentences are correct.

1 Technology **had advanced** _____ by the time I graduate from university.

2 How long **will you have worked** _____ in this industry by the time you retire?

3 The network problem occurred because the IT department **hasn't tested** _____ the software.

4 By 2025, most employees **will be experienced** _____ working in a smart office.

5 Computer viruses **have existed** _____ for many years, but now they are more sophisticated.

6 Within the next three years, most organisations **have installed** _____ some smart technology.

7 We **had already trained** _____ our team on this technology years before any other department became interested.

8 The share price of this technology company **will have increased** _____ recently.

Listening **1** 🔊 4.01 **Listen to a meeting about potential security challenges. Decide if the statements are** *true* **(T) or** *false* **(F).**

1 Angela works for FairWay, an online retail company which sells golfing merchandise. ___

2 Tom is a consultant who advises companies on how to increase customer satisfaction. ___

3 FairWay have recently experienced problems with online hacking. ___

4 Companies similar to FairWay have had issues that affected customers' orders. ___

5 It is possible to install software which would prevent all future cyberattacks. ___

6 Angela is keen to implement any necessary changes quickly. ___

7 FairWay does not have a large amount of money set aside for security. ___

8 Tom will be able to make recommendations by the end of the day. ___

2 **Complete the email with the words in the box. Then listen again to check.**

> analyse costs cyberattacks damage data hacking identify
> improvements network stage systems threats

Dear Angela,

It was good to meet you today. Here is a summary of the main points we discussed. I have also attached an estimate of [1]_____ for each stage of the project in a separate document.

Client's main concerns:
Companies similar to FairWay have experienced recent [2]_____ .
Examples have included [3]_____ or attacks on their computer [4]_____ .
FairWay therefore wishes to be assured that its customers' [5]_____ is secure.
Security [6]_____ are constantly changing and FairWay wants to avoid any [7]_____ to their brand.

Suggested steps:
TW to
- [8]_____ types of cyberattacks taking place in the online retail industry.
- [9]_____ which could pose the greatest threat to FairWay.
- check FairWay's current security [10]_____ and make recommendations for [11]_____ where required.

Time frame:
The analysis and recommendation [12]_____ to be completed by end of the week (June 21st).

Kind regards,
Tom Winterson

3 **Decide if the opinion summaries apply to** *Angela* **(A),** *Tom* **(T) or** *neither of them* **(N).**

1 Believes a recent technology update will help avoid potential challenges. ___

2 Thinks that cybersecurity is essential in keeping a competitive advantage. ___

3 Voices concern that cyberthreats have become increasingly complex. ___

4 Feels that attacks to online transactions is the main issue that needs to be tackled. ___

Functional language

Managing challenging negotiations

1 Choose the correct response.

1 These changes were made after we had briefed the designer.

    a For this precise reason, we haven't got time to go over the details again.

    b We totally understand that you weren't aware of these amendments.

2 Surely we could find some way to cut costs on materials?

    a There's no way we could do that and still retain quality.

    b To put it simply, the initial plans didn't allow for logistics problems.

3 Can you give us a reason for why you're against this approach?

    a Let me tell you what we can do.

    b For one thing, it is way above our agreed budget.

4 But I've already spoken to the supplier and asked him to change materials.

    a I can see that this puts you in a difficult position.

    b It's in all our interests to analyse the research effectively.

5 I'm afraid we were unable to agree to the terms that were suggested.

    a Let's put our heads together and see if we can find an alternative.

    b Besides that, the management will never agree to renewing the contract.

2 Match the correct response (1–5) in Exercise 1 with the strategy (a–c).

a Gives clear reasons for saying 'no'   ___ , ___

b Shows empathy or mutual understanding   ___ , ___

c Explores options and what you can say 'yes' to   ___

Managing challenging conversations

3 Complete the sentences with the words in the box.

benefits correctly elaborate matter objectively overlooking point unreasonable

A I heard that you were upset about not being selected to lead the project?   _1_

A The fact of the [1]_____ is that we would need to see how the training goes. After the course we could discuss potential projects that might be a good fit for you.   ___

A I get your [2]_____ , but this is a very different type of team. It would be useful for you to have further leadership training to help you enter into the role confidently.   ___

A Do you mean in terms of arranging the course? Sure. Come and speak to me tomorrow and we'll look at the best way to proceed.   ___

A I understand that you're disappointed, but can we look at this [3]_____ for a moment? You haven't yet developed the management skills a role like this requires.   ___

B Are you perhaps [4]_____ the fact that I managed teams in my previous position?   ___

B That's right. Could you [5]_____ on why I wasn't considered suitable?   ___

B That doesn't sound [6]_____ . Can we discuss some logical next steps?   ___

B OK, I can see the [7]_____ of what you're saying. And if I follow you [8]_____ , you mean that if I agree to additional training, you'll consider me ready to lead a project?   ___

4 Put the conversation in Exercise 3 into the correct order (1–9). The first line has been done for you.

Writing Proposals – Recommendations

1 Choose the correct option in italics to complete the short business proposal.

Recommendations

Taking all the factors mentioned into account, it appears that there are several ¹*causes / courses / considerations* of action we can take to make our office systems more effective. Having considered all the ²*options / opinions / organisations*, a reasonable ³*account / advice / approach* would be to carry out further research as to which digital strategies might be suitable. In addition, we should ⁴*inform / investigate / involve* ways to make our current administrative procedures more efficient. Some of the recent problems we have experienced are a result of supervisors being unaware of updated data regulations. Therefore, I ⁵*recommend / promote / plan* that all key staff are given additional training in the new processes and procedures. It would also be ⁶*considerable / reasonable / advisable* to take immediate action to look ⁷*out / on / into* ways to improve communication. For example, information is not always shared effectively between management and the workforce. As a result, employees do not feel that their opinions are taken into consideration when changes are made to working practices. ⁸*Consequently / Further / Finally*, we propose to carry out a series of staff consultations on this topic over the next four weeks.

2 Write a short proposal of about 225 words, making recommendations. Use the notes below and the functional language from Exercise 2 on page 46 of the coursebook.

Time management investigation

Options: who will investigate?

Choose from:
- Hire a consultant on a temporary contract
- Use a team from HR to carry out the research

Steps required
- Investigate effectiveness of current work patterns
- Staff to identify issues that affect efficiency in their role – How? Staff survey? Consultations?
- Improve staff engagement – examples?

Recent issues
- Changes made to staff rotas without warning – complaints

Recommendations/actions
- New procedures – give advance warning on any rota changes
- Use online tools for project management – staff access to deadlines/schedules
- Additional time management training – Who for? When?

3 Which summary best describes the viewpoint of the writer in Exercise 1?

a A number of different solutions are possible, but the preferred option is to hire a consultant to train staff to follow procedures.

b Every member of staff needs to be informed that they must follow regulations and must improve administrative procedures.

c The issues were due to lack of knowledge amongst a group of employees, but there is an additional problem related to how information is transferred within the organisation.

Vocabulary Relocation and secondment

1 Complete the text with the words in the box.

> brief   claim   deposit   developmental   international   mobility   perspective   settle

Working across borders

Secondments to overseas offices are an increasingly common occurrence. Employees can enjoy the ¹_____ opportunities that are offered within organisations with a(n) ²_____ network and get a personal ³_____ of how the company works in different regions. It is therefore vital to ⁴_____ staff who are going to work in another country so that they clearly understand their role. When an employee is on secondment, they get the support of a global ⁵_____ team and are often allocated one of their new colleagues as a 'buddy', whose role is to support them as they ⁶_____ into their new life. Secondees may also need help with things such as how to ⁷_____ expenses, find an apartment and pay a ⁸_____ on the property.

Word building – verbs, nouns and adjectives

2 Complete the sentences with the correct form of the word in brackets.

1 All new employees have to complete a special _____ . (assign)

2 HR _____ the 'buddy' team to look after the new secondees. (mobile)

3 The global mobility team helped me to organise the _____ of my belongings. (ship)

4 The company is discussing the _____ of a new secondment policy. (adopt)

5 These earnings are _____ in the secondee's own country. (tax)

6 The company was reluctant to make _____ payments to customers. (compensate)

3 Use the clues to complete the crossword.

Across

1 someone who goes to another country to live there permanently

3 to replace or balance the effect of something bad

4 to give someone a particular job to do

6 a series of actions that are done in order to achieve a particular result

7 the action of moving to a different place

8 the ability to move easily from one job or area to another

Down

2 the process of operating a business in many countries around the world

5 to send goods somewhere by ship, plane, truck, etc.

Grammar   Inversion

1 **Choose the two options which can complete each sentence.**

1   ___ has this industry experienced such outstanding results.

    a Seldom   **b** No sooner   **c** Rarely

2   ___ did we realise there was a major error in the contract.

    a Not until   **b** Only later   **c** Little

3   ___ did we give up hope that a solution could be found.

    a At no time   **b** Not once   **c** Only when

4   Not only would this increase productivity, ___ improve staff motivation.

    a but it could also   **b** could it also   **c** also it could

5   ___would I agree to this relocation package for my team.

    a Not only   **b** On no account   **c** Under no circumstances

2 **Complete the sentences with the words in the box.**

> are   did   had   have   should   will

1   The offer is not very good. Under no circumstances _____ you accept it.

2   The new interns are great. Rarely _____ we had such a talented group.

3   At no time in our last meeting _____ we promise you an increase in salary.

4   Not only _____ they late, but they also haven't phoned to warn us.

5   Only by taking this opportunity _____ you reach your career potential.

6   No sooner _____ they agreed to the relocation package than the offer was withdrawn.

3 **Put the phrases in the correct order to make sentences using inversion.**

1   did she believe / first place / not until she / received the letter / she had won

    _____

2   are given more / make a decision / information can we / only if we

    _____

3   about to fall / little did we know / prices were / that property

    _____

4   circumstances would we / under no / to be an acceptable offer / consider this

    _____

5   did they give / him any feedback / not once / on his performance

    _____

6   a compromise can / job security / only by finding / we guarantee

    _____

7   convincing presentation / seldom have / such a / we heard

    _____

8   but they also / he get an interview, / not only did / offered him the job

    _____

Listening

1 🔊 5.01 **Listen to a podcast about managing a company relocation. Which of the following are mentioned?**

1 family	☐	**5** language training	☐
2 flexible working hours	☐	**6** loneliness	☐
3 mentor support	☐	**7** accommodation	☐
4 financial compensation	☐	**8** cultural issues	☐

2 Listen again and choose the correct option.

1 Which type of relocation is the main focus of the podcast?

  a An organisation relocating to a different base along with most of the staff.

  b Small groups of workers moving as part of a short-term contract.

  c Individual employees moving to another country for their company.

2 According to Alyn, the chance to work and live in another country

  a is every employee's ambition.

  b may not excite every employee.

  c presents a lot of problems for employees.

3 Alyn says that companies may lose good staff if

  a employees are sensitive to changes.

  b the employee's point of view is unclear.

  c the relocation is not managed well.

4 To ensure successful relocation, companies should

  a send employees with their partners and/or families.

  b check that everyone knows what to expect.

  c have a flexible relocation strategy.

5 Alyn says the high costs involved are

  a needed in order to keep the best staff.

  b justified if the employee is valuable.

  c due to staff returning home too soon.

6 Alyn believes that, when relocating staff, companies should

  a prioritise single people.

  b only send people with a good support network.

  c choose the employee best suited for the role.

7 In conclusion, Alyn agrees that a successful relocation depends on

  a an awareness of potential problems.

  b collecting feedback only at the end of the secondment.

  c ensuring employees understand the requirements of the company.

3 Complete the summary with the words in the box. There are three extra words. Look at the audioscript on page 61, if necessary.

avoid   effect   fail   financial   link   personal   purpose   retain   valuable   vital

There is a(n) ¹_____ between relocation and retention of key staff so it is ²_____ that a company has an excellent relocation strategy. If companies ³_____ to prepare both employees and their ⁴_____ support networks of partners or families properly, it can have a devastating ⁵_____ on both the retention of that employee and a company's ⁶ _____ resources. Excellent preparation and communication between company and employee, together with support from colleagues in the other country, will help companies ⁷_____ potential problems.

Functional language

Talking about performance

1 **Choose the correct option in italics to complete the performance review.**

M: What do you like most about your role?

E: I think the most [1]*consistent / rewarding* aspect of my job is finding solutions to client problems. I love that.

M: I can see that. You've provided strong [2]*evidence / thoughts* of that in the really good feedback you've received from clients. You consistently [3]*keep / demonstrate* an ability to come up with creative solutions. You [4]*respond / lead* quickly to rapidly-changing situations and you've also [5]*excelled / failed* at making sure everything runs smoothly at our recent sales conferences.

E: Thank you. I appreciate this positive feedback.

M: However, there are a couple of things that could be better. Firstly, you don't always [6]*follow / keep* the instructions set out in the sales handbook, so I suggest you look at it again.

E: I will.

M: Secondly, you do have [7]*an initiative / a tendency* to be late with your weekly reports. There's definitely [8]*space / room* for improvement there. What do you think you could do to [9]*focus / improve* on that?

E: Well, I think I need to be better at time management. I've been looking into the possibility of going on a time management course and I'd like to hear your [10]*thoughts / priorities* on that.

M: Well, you've certainly [11]*achieved / demonstrated* everything else we've asked of you so I'm sure we can arrange that for you.

E: Thanks.

Developing a convincing argument

2 **Complete the sentences with the phrases in the box.**

> a matter of talking   don't take this opportunity   in a nutshell   one clear benefit
> the obvious thing to do   the twin benefits   the worst

1 _____ of the policy is that it will save a lot of time.

2 _____ now is to ask yourself if you want to move up the career ladder.

3 If you _____ , you will never discover your full potential.

4 _____ , meeting targets determines your future in the company.

5 Even if things don't go well, what's _____ that can actually happen?

6 It's simply _____ to other employees who've already taken the step.

7 This gives you _____ of a bigger team to manage and more responsibility.

3 **Match the sentences (1–7) in Exercise 2 with the functions (a–f).**

a Suggest easy steps for success   ___ , ___

b Highlight the positives   ___

c State two advantages together for impact   ___

d Simplifying to make a clear point   ___

e Emphasise possible lost opportunities   ___

f Reduce negative risks   ___

Writing   Blog post describing relocation

1 Complete the sentences with the words in the box.

> although   beneficial   downside   exchange   expectations
> highly   thanks   understanding

1 _____ to the new relocation strategy, I'm on my way to Johannesburg.

2 I _____ recommend this opportunity to everyone.

3 We believe that secondment is extremely _____ to our employees' careers.

4 The main _____ of the experience is that it can be quite lonely sometimes.

5 She has a much better _____ of how we work now.

6 As part of the company work _____ programme, we are giving junior managers the chance to work in one of our overseas branches.

7 My new job in head office is definitely living up to my _____ .

8 _____ there were some difficulties at first, I now feel really at home here.

2 Complete the table with the correct phrases (1–12).

1 arrived last week

2 company secondment programme

3 started work the next day

4 getting better global perspective

5 interesting work

6 introduced to most staff during day

7 learning to adapt to work culture

8 introduced to manager on first day

9 language difficulties

10 longer working hours

11 recommend it

12 then taken to company apartment

Background information	___
Sequence of events	___ , ___ , ___ , ___ , ___
Pros and cons	___ , ___ , ___ , ___ , ___
Conclusion	___

3 Write a blog post of approximately 225 words about your relocation experience to Shanghai. Include the following:

• the information in Exercise 2.

• functional language from Exercise 1 and page 56 of the coursebook.

• any other information to support the notes.

4 What do you think the main purpose of this blog post is?

a to relate factual information

b to give feedback to the HR department

c to warn employees about the difficulties of relocation

6 > Alliances

Vocabulary   Alliances and acquisitions

1 Complete the text with the words in the box.

> access   gain   outweighed   presence   regulatory   stake   strategic   win-win

There are times when entering into a(n) ¹_____ alliance might be the best option for a company if it wants to ²_____ an advantage over its rivals. But in some cases it may just be the only way to survive in a very competitive market. Our company wanted greater ³_____ to new markets, so working with a company which already had a strong ⁴_____ in those regions was a good way to achieve that. On paper it looked as if it would be a(n) ⁵_____ situation because the benefits far ⁶_____ the costs, but after six months it really wasn't working for us. On reflection we should have considered a joint venture instead, which would only have been for one specific project. Alternatively, we could have accepted the offer from another company which had wanted to have an equity ⁷_____ in our business. That may have saved us numerous headaches. In fact, another of our competitors had previously wanted to take us over, but they didn't get the ⁸_____ approval required so it never happened.

2 Complete the sentences.

1 Our s _ _ _ _ _ _ _ _ _ _ s are delighted with the company's success as their dividends have increased substantially year on year.

2 The best way forward was to engage in a j _ _ _ t v _ _ _ _ _ e with one of our competitors for the latest project.

3 We have just announced the t _ _ _ _ _ _ r of our main rival. This is the start of a new era for the company.

4 The alliance allows us to benefit from greater efficiency and s _ _ _ _ _ y.

5 The a _ _ _ _ _ _ _ _ _ n of our supplier has led to increased productivity in all areas.

3 Choose the correct option in italics to complete the text.

The new alliance allows us to ¹*share / work / provide* our knowledge and ²*presence / resources / ventures* with each other and we find that this is of great ³*benefit / advantage / strength* to both companies. We are able to build a ⁴*stake / synergy / foundation* for expanding our network and therefore creating more business opportunities for both organisations. In fact, we expect a dramatic ⁵*acquisition / approval / turnaround* of fortunes in the coming year.

Grammar Past modals

1 **Choose the correct option in italics. There may be more than one possible answer.**

1 The negotiation *should / must / ought to* have started earlier because now we don't have enough time to discuss all the issues.

2 Both companies *could / ought to / shouldn't* have agreed mutually beneficial goals to avoid this conflict.

3 The company *must / should / couldn't* have arranged the emergency meeting last week because the CEO wasn't available then.

4 The clients were extremely embarrassed – you *couldn't / shouldn't / mustn't* have forgotten their names during the introductions.

5 Philip *couldn't / ought not to / can't* have given the press details of the alliance because he hasn't even seen the file.

6 The manager *may / must / can't* have told the staff about the changes, but I'm not sure.

2 **Put the phrases in the correct order to make sentences.**

1 the project / have expected / with such an inexperienced team / to run smoothly / she couldn't

_____

2 any decisions / have discussed / the merger before / we ought to / were made

_____

3 the airport / because he's just / he can't have / called me from / lost his phone

_____

4 consulting their / have signed / lawyer first / the contract without / they shouldn't

_____

5 have forgotten to / in your diary / make a note / of the deadline / you might

_____

6 due to start / late as we were / must have run / ten minutes ago / their previous appointment / this meeting

_____

3 **Complete the sentences with the past form of the modals in the box.**

can't go   couldn't write   may decide   might find   must agree   should respond

1 I think we should call lost property because someone _____ your wallet after you dropped it in the seminar.

2 I _____ the report earlier because the figures weren't available until today.

3 The shareholders _____ to the alliance or we would have heard otherwise by now.

4 Tina and Gino _____ straight to the apartment because neither of them has the keys.

5 Ursula planned to work late today so she _____ to go straight to the restaurant and meet us there rather than come home first.

6 The client _____ to my previous email about the new designs. Perhaps she doesn't like them.

IS A STRATEGIC ALLIANCE THE BEST WAY TO GO?

As a Management Consultant specialising in strategic alliances and acquisitions, it never ceases to amaze me how many alliances fall at the first hurdle. So, before you decide to follow this path, make sure you read this blog post.

A number of studies indicate that less than 50 percent of all strategic alliances live up to original expectations, something I know from my own experience. [1]___ Unfortunately, many companies only focus on their own desired goals, such as increasing their revenue, rather than on how to achieve these objectives in today's fast-changing world.

So, when a company decides to look for a strategic alliance, it should outline clearly what it wants from that alliance. The key to success is a collaborative working relationship between the two companies. [2]___ This is done by highlighting the differences and creating a shared strategy. There is nothing worse than two companies with different work cultures refusing to change the way they work.

The senior managers need to drive this collaboration and lead by example. To do this, they may have to think outside the box. [3]___ Managers have to realise that alliances require a different kind of thinking because, in reality, the two companies are still competitors, but they are also cooperating with each other.

One company I was working with entered into an alliance with a bigger competitor. Initially, it seemed that they would benefit greatly from an increased customer base and entry into new markets. However, the R&D department had developed an innovative material and they were worried about sharing this confidential information with their partner. Without openness and trust the alliance was bound to fail. It soon became obvious that this was the key reason why the other company had wanted to enter into the alliance in the first place. [4]___ We should have realised that the partner's size might have been an obstacle for us.

Interdependency is the mainstay of any alliance, and interaction between employees should be seamless. [5]___ Joint decisions about recruitment and deployment of staff should be made so that the right person for each job is selected rather than each company favouring their own employees. Furthermore, teams need to follow the same procedures, otherwise a lack of clarity will lead to inevitable confusion, inefficiency and, ultimately, failure.

In conclusion, do not rush into an alliance without agreeing to every operational policy beforehand, otherwise you may become one more statistic in the list of those who have fallen at the first fence.

1 Read and complete the blog post with sentences A–F. There is one extra sentence.

A Several meetings took place but neither side was able to agree on how to move forward.

B So, from the outset it is crucial to understand each other's organisation.

C Remaining in their comfort zones should not be an option.

D Consequently, a combined alliance strategy should be agreed before finalising the details of the alliance so that everyone knows what the framework is.

E Owing to the fact that they were much bigger than us, we ended up having to follow their procedures and were outnegotiated in most decisions.

F I have worked in several companies over the past few years and can confirm that there are obvious pitfalls when embarking on this strategy, but these can be avoided.

2 Complete the notes with words from the blog post.

Strategic alliances	
Advantages	Having access to new [1]_____
	Improving the amount of [2]_____
	Gaining a larger customer [3]_____
Keys for success	Encouraging a working relationship that is [4]_____
	Recognising the [5]_____ in each company
	Honesty and [6]_____ between the two organisations
Potential problems	Only concentrating on own [7]_____
	Failing to follow new [8]_____
	Being unwilling to share [9]_____ information

3 What is the purpose of the blog post?

a to explain how a strategic alliance works

b to advise on the best way to approach an alliance

c to give examples of the pitfalls of strategic alliances

Functional language

Diffusing conflict

1 Complete the dialogue with the phrases in the box.

if we were to   I'll agree to set up   let's figure out   most concerns me   potential problem   reach a compromise   straight to the point   to raise the issues   you be prepared

A: So let's get [1]_____ . We need to meet up with our potential alliance partner as soon as possible.

B: I know, but what [2]_____ is that we'll make the same mistakes as with our previous alliance. Remember how that ended?

A: Not if we plan it more carefully. What [3]_____ create a checklist for us to discuss with them? Would [4]_____ to do that this week?

B: Yes, good idea. I'll get a first draft to you by tomorrow.

C: The [5]_____ I see is that we haven't really got much time. We should have done this far earlier.

A: I know, but we didn't. There's no time for regrets now so [6]_____ our approach to the discussions as quickly as possible.

C: We can't let them dictate to us how the new alliance would operate.

A: Too right! So [7]_____ a meeting with the potential partner, then. Is that OK with everyone?

B: Absolutely. We definitely need [8]_____ that we're worried about before we agree to anything.

A: Agreed. We need a joint policy on everything. I'm sure we'll be able to [9]_____ that suits us all.

Analysing and learning from mistakes

2 Choose the correct option in italics to complete the dialogue.

A: Entering into an alliance has been quite good for the most part. However, in many [1]*approaches / ways,* our biggest mistake was not getting regular feedback from staff.

B: I agree. This [2]*meant / considered* that we didn't realise how unhappy they were because of the confusion about procedural guidelines.

A: I know. With [3]*reference / hindsight,* we should have realised this earlier. If we'd spent more time in the planning stages, we might have avoided losing some of our best staff.

B: Exactly. One thing I hadn't [4]*created / expected* was how demotivated they would become because of the lack of clear guidelines.

A: And, of course, it wasn't [5]*addressed / foreseen* that we wouldn't be able to increase salaries this year due to the recession.

B: We couldn't have planned for that. I think the key [6]*takeaway / hindsight* for me here is that we need to ensure that all employees are following the correct company procedures.

A: So, we need to write new guidelines immediately and schedule in regular feedback from all staff.

B: Nevertheless, all [7]*in / for* all, we haven't done too badly, despite this problem.

A: Agreed. [8]*Considering / Thinking* everything that happened, we did OK and going [9]*forward / future,* I'd like us to offer staff more training and support.

B: I'm in total agreement.

Writing   Report extract

1 Complete the report extract with the words in the box.

> clear   discussion   failure   hope   lack   result

In the ¹_____ of increasing revenue we have decided to enter into a strategic alliance. We have been in ²_____ with our main competitor and believe that this is the best way forward for both companies. The ³_____ of new sales over the past year and a ⁴_____ to break into the South American markets, where our partner already has a strong presence, has left this company in a very weak position. It is ⁵_____ that these markets are not easy to access without expert help, so this is an excellent way for us to expand into those markets. Agreement on all details has not yet been reached but we anticipate that this will happen in the next month. As a ⁶_____ of this proposed alliance, we are currently considering ways to restructure our company to bring it more in line with that of our partner.

2 Complete the second sentence so that it means the same as the first. Use two to five words, including the word in brackets.

1 We are doing this because we think it will expand the business.

We are doing this _____ the business. (hope)

2 I see very few benefits for us to agree to this alliance.

There _____ for us in going ahead with this alliance. (advantage)

3 We can definitely see a huge benefit of working with that company.

It _____ a huge benefit of working with that company. (evident)

4 We made the decision because of these issues.

For _____ , we made the decision. (reasons)

5 We don't think that the problem is with the software.

The problem _____ with the software. (appear)

3 Write a report extract of about 225 words. Use the notes below and add any other information.

> - new contract to build 2,000 homes over the next two years – must meet deadlines = possible strategic alliance with main supplier – close to an agreement
> - reasons:
>   1) expansion: smooth supply chain = no delays = meet deadline
>   2) shared kills, knowledge, expertise
> - needs: close working relationship, good communication, defined procedures / job roles = more future projects

4 Who do you think the report is for? Tick (✓) all that apply.

a the shareholders ☐

b the supplier ☐

c the general public ☐

d the chief executive ☐

e potential investors ☐

f the board of directors ☐

Vocabulary Managing and minimising risk

1 Complete the sentences with the words in the box.

disaster   measures   mitigated   pose   solutions   stock   suffered   thinking

1 We need some forward _____ now to anticipate possible problems in the next five years.

2 Do you think that the problem in that market could _____ a threat to our sales?

3 The company took preventive _____ when they realised the potential problems facing them.

4 The building _____ a lot of damage during the fire last week.

5 We have _____ the environmental risk of this project.

6 We are going to test the _____ to this problem to ensure we are getting the results we need.

7 Our problems are reflected on the _____ market as the value of our shares has gone down.

8 The company prevented a _____ by finding a new partner who was able to turn the business around.

2 Use the clues to complete the crossword.

Across

4 If there is a danger to you, you … at risk.

6 Something that may be dangerous is a … risk.

7 You take precautionary measures to … the risk.

Down

1 To do something although you know you might fail is to … a risk.

2 To limit a risk as much as possible is to … the risk.

3 A carefully worked out, or analysed, risk is a … risk.

5 A very serious risk is a … risk.

3 Complete the words in the text. The first letter of each word is given.

While completing a risk ¹a _ _ _ _ _ _ _ for the trade fair venue, we discovered that there were several areas which could be dangerous for staff and visitors to the trade fair once the equipment was set up. We therefore assessed all the ²h _ _ _ _ _ _ in order to ³m _ _ _ _ _ these risks and ⁴p _ _ _ _ _ _ potential disasters. We have changed some of the layout of the equipment and HR have organised specific training for the staff attending the fair. We need to make sure that we don't ⁵r _ _ the risk of causing any accidents to visitors.

Grammar   Second, third and mixed conditionals

1 **Match the sentences (1–8) with the type of conditional (a–d).**

1 If he'd spoken to an advisor, he could have invested his money in a safer industry.

2 We wouldn't have such good results if we didn't take some risks.

3 If the shareholders hadn't agreed to their proposals, the company wouldn't be as successful.

4 If it weren't so difficult to raise funds, we'd have opened another branch by now.

5 Their shareholders would have been upset if they'd made further losses.

6 He might have his own business now if he'd taken a few more risks.

7 She wouldn't have been promoted if she wasn't such a great team leader.

8 If you attended the meetings you might understand the issues.

a Second conditional   ___ , ___

b Third conditional   ___ , ___

c Mixed conditional (present consequence of past action)   ___ , ___

d Mixed conditional (past consequence of present situation) ___ , ___

2 **Choose the correct option to complete the sentences. Use the meaning as a guide.**

1 There wouldn't ___ a financial crisis if the banks had cooperated.

    a have be   **b** had been   **c** have been

2 If he ___ some risks, he wouldn't own such a unique company.

    a has taken   **b** hadn't taken   **c** would take

3 You could have gone to university if you ___ your exams.

    a had passed   **b** would have passed   **c** have had past

4 If you listened to his advice, you ___ something.

    a would have learned   **b** might learn   **c** had learned

5 We wouldn't ___ scientists if we weren't keen on experiments.

    a have become   **b** had become   **c** became

6 If they ___ more research, they wouldn't have lost all their savings.

    a could do   **b** might have done   **c** had done

3 **Cross out the mistake in each sentence and write the correction.**

1 He would have won the Economics prize if he wasn't so good at statistics.
_____

2 If we hadn't employed the right people, we weren't where we are today.
_____

3 If house prices didn't crash, there wouldn't be a financial crisis. _____

4 We could only take on more risk if we would be promised higher returns.
_____

5 If your organisation hadn't become so popular on social media, it doesn't have had such a positive impact. _____

Listening

1 ◀) 7.01 **Listen to five people giving advice about investing in today's uncertain markets. Which speaker (1–5) is talking about:**

a commissioning different people to oversee different investments? ___

b investing in an asset that usually does well in uncertain markets? ___

c a way to balance out investments? ___

d investing in various assets to avoid potentially losing too much? ___

e preventing expensive borrowing? ___

2 **Complete the summary of each speaker's advice with the words in the box. Then listen again and check.**

> assets   economic recovery   emotion   fund managers   inflation   negative effect
> predict   safety net   spending   stocks   strong returns   technology   top   volatile

Speaker 1
- Nearly impossible to ¹_____ which market is going to do well.
- Good diversifier is gold – it performs well in ²_____ markets and when there is ³_____ .

Speaker 2
- Investing money in a single sector can lead to a serious ⁴_____ on finances.
- Should spread investments over different ⁵_____ .
- Can have ⁶_____ from infrastructure trusts.

Speaker 3
- Different ⁷_____ might be required at various times of the economic cycle.
- Growth in ⁸_____ stocks can be remarkable.
- Some experts buy cheaper stocks expecting them to improve in an ⁹_____ .

Speaker 4
- It's important to have a(n) ¹⁰_____ of cash in a weak stock market for short-term ¹¹_____ goals.
- However, cash is not good enough to fund your retirement.

Speaker 5
- Investing smaller amounts of money at a time removes the ¹²_____ from the action.
- Over time, this approach will average out the price you pay for ¹³_____ .
- Risk is limited by selling good investments at the ¹⁴_____ of the market.

3 **Which statement best summarises the overall message of all the speakers?**

a Holding on to expensive investments is a proven key to success.

b It's important to find different ways to beat inflation in an uncertain economy.

c Investors need to look at different ways to diversify their investments.

d Government regulations and decisions can pose a threat to investments.

Functional language

Talking about risk

1 Complete the dialogue with one word in each gap.

A: I think we need to be prepared [1]_____ all eventualities.

B: I agree. The worst [2]_____ scenario is that we lose the contract. And that's a big deal.

A: It is. So, before the meeting we need to gather as much information as possible.

B: But that would be very [3]_____-consuming and expensive. The deadline's too short.

A: Yes, but we need to [4]_____ the unexpected. If we're prepared for anything, that will [5]_____ us more confidence.

B: That's true, but if we know our business well enough, we'll be able to deal with any issues as they [6]_____ .

A: Do you think I'm being [7]_____?

B: Possibly. You're right, we do need to be aware of potential problems – that way we can [8]_____ all bases, but just not in great detail.

A: OK. I hope you're right.

Analysing risks

2 Choose the correct option in italics to complete the sentences.

1 There's a medium level of *probability / method / radar* that it will happen. But if it does, we'll be prepared.

2 What *effect / probability / methods* would we use to analyse the risks we're facing?

3 This will likely *range / cause / establish* us a delay in manufacturing if we don't do something now.

4 There's *a catastrophic / an urgent / a possible* need to deal with this issue as soon as possible.

5 From our analysis we have *caused / mitigated / identified* two main areas of risk.

6 I think that some of the problems may not be on our *impact / radar / plan*.

3 Match the sentences (1–6) in Exercise 2 with the functions (a–d).

a Talking about risk analysis ___ , ___

b Identifying risks ___

c Talking about probability and possible outcomes ___ , ___

d Deciding on action ___

Writing Accident report

1 Complete the headings in the accident report with the words and phrases in the box.

> analysis causes date details how to avoid injuries involved recommendations

Accident report

Facts	
Person(s) ¹_____	
²_____ , time and location	
Full ³_____ of incident	
⁴_____ and treatment	
⁵_____	
⁶_____ of incident	
⁷_____	
⁸_____ it in future	

2 Complete the email with the correct form of the verbs in brackets.

Date: 10 October

From: Ben Donlight, Warehouse Manager

To: Enya Milner, Human Resources Manager

Subject: Accident in warehouse

Natasha Bellini, one of our warehouse workers ¹_____ (injure) at 9 a.m. this morning, while she ²_____ (lift) a very heavy box from a high shelf. She dropped the box on her foot and also ³_____ (hurt) her back. She ⁴_____ (check) by the company nurse who sent her to hospital. Consequently, she ⁵_____ (not / be) able to work for at least two weeks. I ⁶_____ (just / fill) out the accident report, which you ⁷_____ (find) on the system. We need ⁸_____ (remind) staff about the health and safety rules and regulations, so please can we arrange more regular training for them?

Many thanks,

Ben

3 Read the notes below and complete the accident report in Exercise 1. Write about 225 words. Invent any other information required.

- *Jack Roberts, metal worker – engineering plant A – Thursday 7th July – 11.30 a.m.*
- *working on engine – turned quickly and tripped over equipment left on floor by another worker*
- *twisted ankle – cut head – hospital check*

Vocabulary   Decisions

1 Choose the correct option in italics to complete the sentences.

1 Our innovation is *driving / examining / pulling* our current success.

2 We have now *developed / collected / settled* all the information needed to make a decision.

3 We've *examined / identified / listed* the feedback from our customers and have decided to make certain changes.

4 It's vital that we *settle / identify / define* the best alternative available at this moment.

5 We have *reconsidered / established / defined* our decision and concluded that we need to find an alternative solution.

6 The authorities have *evaluated / identified / given* the go-ahead for the takeover.

7 They failed to *collect / monitor / settle* the solution, which led to disastrous results.

2 Complete the text with the words in the box. There is one extra word.

> ahead   alternative   ending   forward   gut   making   pulling   settle

> Decision-1_____ can be very tough at times and it's been hard to know what to do. However, I think that now the only way 2_____ for the company is to look for a strategic alliance partner. My 3_____ feeling is that it won't be easy to find one, but I don't think we have any choice. We must stop arguing about the situation and start 4_____ together if we are going to make the right decision. We're in danger of 5_____ up losing a lot of market share if we don't go down this path. I don't want to 6_____ on a decision that I think is a poor compromise. Consequently, I now believe that out of all the 7_____ options, the best one is a strategic alliance.

3 Complete the sentences.

1 We need to e __ __ l __ __ __ e our solution and make sure that it is working well.

2 We i __ __ l __ __ __ __ n __ __ d the plan of action as quickly as possible.

3 They didn't c __ __ s __ __ __ __ r all the possible options, which led to the poor decision.

4 Once you have d __ f __ __ __ __ d the problem, then you are able to look at ways to solve it.

5 We made a list of all the c __ __ t __ __ __ __ a before looking for solutions.

6 Unfortunately, there were too many c __ __ s __ __ __ __ n __ s to make that option viable.

7 The company d __ __ e __ o __ __ d a really effective plan of action.

Grammar *to* + infinitive or *-ing* form

1 Choose the correct option in italics to complete the sentences.

1 It would be a mistake to avoid *to make / making* a decision on this matter.

2 The board of directors has decided *to hold / holding* an enquiry.

3 We have put off *to discuss / discussing* this issue for long enough.

4 The management team promises *to consider / considering* all suggestions.

5 The consultants would like *to speak / speaking* to all staff about this.

6 We apologise for *to keep / keeping* you waiting.

2 Complete the text with the correct form of the verbs in brackets.

The management team is afraid of ¹_____ (take) the wrong decision
at this point in time. They're very good at ²_____ (come) up with new
ideas and strategies, but times are so uncertain at the moment that they might
decide ³_____ (do) nothing at all. However, it is clear that they need
⁴_____ (make) a decision of some kind if they hope
⁵_____ (survive) this economic downturn. I remember
⁶_____ (have) the same problem a few years ago at the company I was
working for then. They didn't stop ⁷_____ (think) about the whole economic
situation and ended up ⁸_____ (not make) any decisions and failing as
a result. The team must be strong and think about ⁹_____ (weigh) up all the
pros and cons. Then they must insist on ¹⁰_____ (create) a plan for moving
forward as quickly as possible.

3 Match the sentence beginnings (1–8) with the correct ending (a or b).

1 They managed ___

2 I need ___

3 I'm afraid that option means ___

4 They offered ___

5 We regret ___

6 It was not worth ___

7 The assistant almost forgot ___

8 They tried really hard ___

a to rearrange the meeting.

b taking that pay cut.

Reading

Is courage the key to good business decisions?

'Whenever you see a successful business, someone once made a courageous decision.' — Peter F. Drucker

A

Successful business decisions have been analysed and dissected a multitude of times in an attempt to provide a roadmap for effective decision-making. So, why is it that so many people are still frightened of making the wrong decision? They seem to have forgotten that you can only make the best decision you can with the knowledge you have at any one point, and it can only then be declared a good decision further down the line if the required results are achieved.

B

All decision-making by nature involves a certain amount of risk because no one can accurately predict the future. An individual can try to limit those risks by assessing all the factors surrounding each decision, but many external factors are out of their control, especially in today's globally connected businesses. What is happening on the other side of the world can affect a business thousands of miles away. Decision-makers, therefore, need to accept that they may never make a perfect decision.

C

As Drucker observed, business leaders sometimes have to make *courageous* decisions. Nevertheless, these should not be confused with making rushed or reckless decisions – it should be a calculated risk. Moreover, successful decision-makers are not scared of making mistakes, instead they learn from them. They maintain a positive outlook even when things do not go according to plan, and are able to pick themselves up and quickly find ways of resolving the situation.

D

Successful decision-makers do not shy away from making a difficult decision, and they do not worry about losing face if a problem arises as a result of one of their decisions. Good decision-makers are constantly looking for the root cause of any problem and seeking to find a real solution and not just a temporary fix. They consider the health of their organisation first, rather than their own image or reputation.

E

Today, the pace of change is faster than ever before and people may feel under pressure to make decisions more quickly than they would like. However, there is much more information available at the touch of a button so there is no excuse to be out of touch with what is happening globally. Decision-makers need to use all the knowledge at their disposal, but without becoming overloaded with irrelevant information.

1 Read the article quickly. Which paragraph mentions:

1 putting the business before the individual?   ____

2 remaining optimistic at all times?   ____

3 assessing the success of a decision?   ____

4 utilising all available data?   ____

5 understanding the impact of the global economy?   ____

2 Read the article again and decide if these statements are *true* (T) or *false* (F).

1 Many business people often lack confidence when making important decisions.   ____

2 Good decision-makers know their decision will always lead to the desired outcome. ____

3 The interconnectivity of global business makes it more difficult to make decisions with certainty.   ____

4 Making quick decisions is the sign of a good decision-maker.   ____

5 Good decision-makers are not concerned about how people will judge them if they end up making a bad decision.   ____

6 Good decision-makers are only concerned with short-term solutions.   ____

7 Decision-makers have to be selective about what information to consider.   ____

3 What is the purpose of the article?

a to explain why some people cannot make good decisions

b to encourage decision-makers to take more risks

c to demonstrate how successful decision-makers operate

Functional language

Fact-based and emotion-based approaches to decision-making

1 Complete the dialogue with the words and phrases in the box.

black and white   cloud   even though   instinct would be   lack of
of the matter   our feelings   personally   true that

A: Well, that was a tricky meeting, wasn't it?

B: It was. The fact ¹_____ is there was a definite ²_____ cooperation with the suppliers, wasn't there?

A: I agree, and I ³_____ still feel a bit worried about working with them. I'm not sure we can entirely trust them.

B: I know what you mean, but we can't let ⁴_____ about the previous encounter with them ⁵_____ our judgement. Just because they messed us around last year, it doesn't mean they will again this time. And their prices are much cheaper than our current supplier.

A: I suppose you're right. However, my ⁶_____ to have another meeting with them and explain our situation again. What do you think?

B: That sounds like a good idea. It's ⁷_____ we have had problems before so we do need to clear the air.

A: Exactly. And then, when we agree the contract, we'll have all the details and agreements in ⁸_____ so we all know where we stand.

B: Yes, ⁹_____ the negotiations may take longer than expected, I'm sure that we'll finally come to an agreement that is workable for all concerned.

Relationship-oriented decision-making

2 Complete the dialogue with one word in each gap.

A: We both know that the joint venture is good for both our companies and we ¹_____ good intentions when we first started these negotiations, didn't we?

B: Absolutely. We both want it to be a successful collaboration. So, what's the problem from your viewpoint?

A: There's no easy ²_____ to say this, so I'll just say it. I'm afraid we can't agree to the project schedule as it stands at the moment.

B: OK. Well, we can sort this out. I'm sure we'd both like to find a quick resolution ³_____ we can keep both our interests in focus. But I thought you were happy with the schedule?

A: I was at first. Initially, it looked ⁴_____ a good plan, but with hindsight, I don't think you've given us enough time to complete each section. I don't want to cause any hostility ⁵_____ us so do you think we can ⁶_____ beyond this?

B: Of course we can. Future collaboration is in both of our ⁷_____ .

A: That's great.

B: Do you have an ⁸_____ with anything else other than the deadlines? I need to get a ⁹_____ for your concerns before I can address them.

A: Well, there are a few other details I'd like to discuss.

B: Sure. In that case, let's put the final decision on ¹⁰_____ for a week to give you time to send me your suggestions for changes. We'll meet again after that to finalise the schedule. How does that sound?

A: That works for me, thanks for your understanding.

Writing   Describing a decision

1 Complete the excerpts from a formal letter with the words in the box. There are two extra words.

> assure   be improved   cause   consider   enable   guarantee   result   view

---

The new factory will ¹_____ us to meet the increased demand for the new lines.
Both efficiency and productivity will ²_____ .

We ³_____ you that no staff will be forced to relocate. In addition, we can
⁴_____ that our existing customers will not be adversely affected during this process.

In ⁵_____ of this decision, we are planning to recruit twenty new members of staff.
The company will also ⁶_____ offering employees a comprehensive health package.

---

2 Which of the introductory sentences (a–c) would be most appropriate for the formal letter in Exercise 1?

a

Dear Mr Kiebel,

I'm writing to tell you about the meeting last week and the decision we made. As you know, we want to have a bigger factory so we're going to build one because of all the orders we are going to get.

b

Dear Mr Kiebel,

Further to our recent discussion about increasing production capacity, it has been decided to build a new factory. This will enable us to meet the expected demands of our order book for the new product lines.

c

Dear Mr Kiebel,

I'm glad to tell you that, as a result of our meeting last week, we have made a big decision to build a new factory. This means we can produce more and keep our customers happy. We believe this is a great decision.

3 Write a formal letter of about 225 words to the Sales and Marketing Manager of your Paris office. Use the notes below and invent any other information required.

- discussion last week – new Sales and Marketing office in Rome / fast-growing market / Paris office currently responsible for Italy
- Rome office – better relationship with Italian clients / need face-to-face contact in Italy / help increase market share
- possible period of readjustment for Paris office / promise no redundancies
- 6-month secondment for 2 Paris employees / oversee setting up

Pronunciation

Unit 1

1.2 Intonation in question tags

1 🔊 P1.01 **Listen to the question tags. Are the people asking a question or just checking?**

		Asking	Checking
1	Something's wrong here, isn't it?	☐	☐
2	Nobody's joining us, are they?	☐	☐
3	Please call later, will you?	☐	☐
4	Let's get started, shall we?	☐	☐
5	Everyone lives in the area, don't they?	☐	☐
6	Nothing's clear in this report, is it?	☐	☐
7	We rarely ask general questions in surveys, do we?	☐	☐
8	Someone with less time would have more of a problem, wouldn't they?	☐	☐

2 **Listen again and practise saying the sentences.**

3 **Complete the sentences using question tags and practise saying them.**

1 Participants should try to agree with each other, _____ ? (checking)

2 If it wasn't too expensive, you'd go there sometimes, _____ ? (asking)

3 There isn't anything like this at the moment, _____ ? (checking)

4 It really combines convenience with healthy eating, _____ ? (checking)

5 Participants of focus groups should all be very similar, _____ ? (asking)

6 That seems to be what we all want, _____ ? (asking)

7 Let's see if we can fix it, _____ ? (asking)

8 We're all looking forward to the course, _____? (checking)

4 🔊 P1.02 **Listen and check. Then listen again and repeat the sentences.**

1.3 Indian English pronunciation

1 🔊 P1.03 **Listen and tick (✓) the phrases spoken by an Indian English speaker.**

1	outside the scope	☐	5	when I talked about	☐
2	the main question	☐	6	to be mindful that	☐
3	time to look at	☐	7	the answer to that question	☐
4	about this issue	☐	8	Is that OK?	☐

2 🔊 P1.04 **Listen and complete the sentences.**

1 It's not something _____ have _____ to look at _____ .

2 I'm not _____ sure of the _____ to that question.

3 I'll _____ directly _____ you. Is _____ OK?

4 That question is _____ the scope of today's _____ .

5 We _____ to be _____ that many _____ feel _____ strongly about _____ .

6 We _____ that at the _____ of the presentation when I _____ about ...

7 _____ the main _____ you _____ on this?

8 You'd be better off _____ my _____ in Finance about this _____ .

Unit 2

2.2 Intonation in cleft sentences

1 🔊 P2.01 **Listen and underline the main stresses. The number of stressed words is given in brackets.**

1 What I'll do tomorrow is to make sure the contract is ready. (3)

2 It was the boring work that made him leave. (2)

3 Something they forgot to take was the latest version of the agreement. (2)

4 What we'll have to rethink are our conditions of employment. (3)

5 It's the supplier in Mexico that my boss is trying to reach. (1)

6 The innovation that didn't work was the one that was most expensive. (2)

2 **Listen again and practise saying the sentences.**

3 🔊 P2.02 **Listen and underline the main stresses in part B of the exchanges.**

1 **A:** Have you managed to get through to the supplier in Mexico yet?

 B: It's my boss that's trying to get through to them.

2 **A:** Have you managed to get through to the supplier in Mexico yet?

 B: It's the manufacturer in Mexico I'm trying to reach.

3 **A:** I thought they liked the ideas?

 B: What they criticised was the lack of time to implement them.

4 **A:** I think he left because of the atmosphere in the office, didn't he?

 B: What made him leave was the boring work he had to do.

5 **A:** He says he left because of the boring work.

 B: What made me leave was the atmosphere in the office.

6 **A:** They took various versions of the agreement with them.

 B: Unfortunately, the only one they forgot to take was the latest one.

4 🔊 P2.03 **Listen and practise saying the sentences. You will hear part A of each exchange. Reply with part B.**

2.4 Southern U.S. English pronunciation

1 🔊 P2.04 **Listen and tick (✓) the phrases spoken by a Southern U.S. English speaker.**

1	from your side	☐	**5**	eye to eye	☐
2	you said	☐	**6**	very valid	☐
3	any quick wins	☐	**7**	from the agenda	☐
4	your take on this	☐	**8**	increase the insurance	☐

2 🔊 P2.05 **Listen and complete the sentences.**

1 Do you see _____ quick _____ here?

2 I think both _____ are _____ _____ .

3 Let me make sure we _____ understood what you _____ .

4 Any _____ from your _____ ?

5 We don't really see _____ to _____ on _____ .

6 You can see from the _____ what we're all looking to _____ today.

7 We need to _____ the _____ for the project.

8 What's your _____ on _____ , _____ ?

Unit 3

3.2 Stress in phrasal verbs

1 P3.01 **Listen and underline the stressed words.**

1 She carried on living with her mother.

2 She managed to put some money by each month.

3 She wanted to save up before studying at university.

4 She didn't want to fall behind with the rent.

5 Her grandfather had set up a trust fund for her.

2 Listen again and practise saying the sentences.

3 P3.02 **Listen and underline the stressed words. The number of stressed words is given in brackets.**

1 He set a trust fund up. (2)

2 He set it up. (2)

3 She wanted to save some money up. (2)

4 The problem has come up before. (2)

5 What if your computer breaks down? (1)

6 He wouldn't be able to pay them back. (3)

7 They agreed to pay off his debts. (3)

8 They agreed to pay them off. (2)

4 Listen again and practise saying the sentences.

3.3 Chunking and stress in presentations

1 P3.03 **Listen to part of a presentation and mark the pauses. Then listen again and underline the stressed words.**

Then ... try and visualise the looks on your guests' faces as they enter the ballroom and see more than one hundred circus performers all dressed in gold. Fire acts! Acrobats! Jugglers! Trapeze artists! All surrounded by enormous golden urns with thousands of flowers cascading from them. Imagine how everyone will react to this incredible sight.

2 Listen again and practise reading the presentation with the recording.

3 Practise saying the presentation. Pay attention to the pauses and stresses.

Unit 4

4.2 Weak forms in perfect tenses

1 🔊 P4.01 **Listen and underline the sentence you hear.**

1 How many computers have been affected?   How many computers had been affected?

2 They still haven't recovered.   They still hadn't recovered.

3 The ransomware will be aimed at banks.   The ransomware had been aimed at banks.

4 He said he's been told.   He said he'd been told.

5 They'd chosen their targets carefully.   They've chosen their targets carefully.

6 A UK plant will have been targeted.   A UK plant will be targeted.

2 🔊 P4.02 **Listen and practise saying both sentences in each pair.**

3 🔊 P4.03 **Listen and complete the sentences.**

1 Before I _____ in this office, I _____ at a smart desk.

2 The virus _____ quickly.

3 I _____ this kind of smart building before.

4 By the time I _____ it, it was out of date.

5 I _____ for the company for nearly two years.

6 They thought they _____ , but they _____ , in fact.

7 They still _____ the system back online.

8 They _____ random targets.

9 I'm sure they _____ to respond.

10 I don't think we _____ , _____ we?

11 By the end of the day we _____ all the details.

12 They thought they _____ , but they _____ .

4 **Listen again and practise saying the sentences.**

4.4 Volume and tone of voice in challenging conversations

1 🔊 P4.04 **Listen and repeat part B's responses, trying to sound like the speaker on the recording.**

1 **A:** Experience isn't the only factor we have to take into account.

   B: So, to put it differently, you're saying that my experience didn't matter in this case?

2 **A:** I agree that you both have similar skills and abilities.

   B: But if I follow you correctly, you mean that he was the better person for the job?

3 **A:** I'm sorry that we weren't able to give you the team leader position on this occasion.

   B: The fact of the matter is that I'm a little confused and disappointed not to have got the position.

4 **A:** Of course we've been very impressed by your recent performance.

   B: Yes, can we talk about that for a moment?

5 **A:** He did a very good job on the last project.

   B: But are you perhaps overlooking the fact that he asked for my assistance at several key points?

6 **A:** We have a major new project coming up which you could be involved in.

   B: OK, so what exactly would need to happen to move forward from here?

Unit 5

5.1 Stress patterns in word building

1 Write the words in the correct place in the table according to their stress pattern.

> adopted   assign   assigned   assignment   compensatory   cultural   culture   employ   employee   globalised   globalisation   immigrant   immigration   mobilise   process   processed   relocate   relocated   seconded   shipping   taxable   taxation

Oo	
oO	
Ooo	
oOo	
ooO	
ooOo	
ooOoo	
oooOo	

2 🔊 P5.01 Listen and check. Then listen again and practise saying the words.

3 Write the stress patterns for these words.

1 accommodation _____
2 helpful _____
3 personal _____
4 development _____
5 compensation _____
6 interpreter _____
7 opportunities _____
8 permanently _____
9 organisation _____

4 🔊 P5.02 Listen and check. Then listen again and practise saying the words.

5.2 Stress and intonation in inversions

1 🔊 P5.03 Listen and complete the sentences.

1 _____ get any really exciting opportunities.
2 _____ know how difficult it would be to learn a new language.
3 _____ been treated so badly by an employer.
4 _____ interesting, but I also got to know something of a different culture.
5 _____ offered any kind of support.
6 _____ arrived than she knew she'd be happy there.
7 _____ saying that you were responsible for what happened.
8 _____ sign the contract in its present form.
9 _____ realise what a great experience it had been.
10 _____ have to book a flight, but they also had to find accommodation.
11 _____ the job did he realise it was the opportunity of a lifetime.
12 _____ accept that assignment abroad.

2 Listen again. Practise saying the sentences with the same speed and stress patterns as in the recording.

Unit 6

6.2 Weak forms in past modals

1 ◀) P6.01 **Listen and underline the sentence you hear.**

1 They must be working late.   They must have been working late.

2 You ought to have left the company.   You oughtn't to have left the company.

3 They can't have left on time.   They couldn't have left on time.

4 You should take the other job.   You should have taken the other job.

5 They couldn't have known that the brand would become so popular.

   They can't have known that the brand would become so popular.

2 ◀) P6.02 **Listen and practise saying both sentences in each pair.**

3 ◀) P6.03 **Listen and complete the sentences.**

1 Don't you think we _____ joined forces?

2 We obviously _____ predicted what the results of the merger would be.

3 They _____ kept the brand name, _____ they?

4 There _____ been a lot of different possibilities.

5 They _____ wanted to make use of synergy.

6 _____ left earlier to be on time for your appointment?

7 The company _____ grown faster under different ownership.

8 A strategic alliance _____ been a good idea.

9 _____ taken on the new role you were offered?

10 They _____ told you the details, because they don't know them
   themselves yet.

11 They _____ been trying to decrease competition, _____ they?

12 They say we _____ solved the problem months ago, but I can't see how
   we _____ .

4 **Listen again and practise saying the sentences.**

6.4 Scottish English pronunciation

1 ◀) P6.04 **Listen and tick (✓) the phrases spoken by a Scottish English speaker.**

1 with hindsight   ☐   5 proud of what   ☐

2 main lesson learnt   ☐   6 different versions   ☐

3 roles and responsibilities ☐   7 hadn't expected   ☐

4 the main problem was   ☐   8 what are your   ☐

2 ◀) P6.05 **Listen and complete the sentences.**

1 Considering _____ that _____ I'm very proud of _____ we achieved.

2 In future, _____ and responsibilities should be _____ more _____ .

3 My main _____ learnt is that _____ need to be addressed _____ .

4 With _____ , we should have used a _____ planning tool.

5 One thing I hadn't _____ was that they'd need so much _____ .

6 _____ are your _____ on this?

7 In many ways, I think that the main _____ was a _____ failure.

8 This _____ the _____ that people had different _____ of the schedule.

Unit 7

7.1 Linking between words

1 Before you listen, decide which linking sound you expect to hear: /w/ or /r/.

1 two‿or more floors
2 four‿earthquakes
3 so‿always remember
4 Do you‿always check?
5 more‿emergencies
6 Is this door‿a fire door?
7 better‿equipment
8 for‿emergency use only

2 ◀》P7.01 Listen and check. Then listen again and practise saying the phrases.

3 Before you listen, mark all the possible links in the sentences.

1 Keep the weight of the building as light as possible.
2 Many buildings have to be demolished after earthquakes.
3 Buildings in the capital are more at risk than those in other areas.
4 How do earthquakes affect business and the economy?
5 Have you ever worked in a skyscraper?
6 Fire alarms are an effective means of saving lives.
7 Smart systems automatically reduce risk to people in a building.
8 The lifts stop automatically at the nearest floor.

4 ◀》P7.02 Listen and mark the links you hear. Write /w/ or /r/ and use ‿ for other consonant-vowel links.

5 Listen again and practise saying the sentences.

7.2 Intonation in conditionals

1 ◀》P7.03 Listen and complete the sentences.

1 If he were a _____ , he probably wouldn't have spent his early childhood _____ .

2 If he hadn't decided to pursue a _____ , he wouldn't have gravitated _____ .

3 If it hadn't been for a _____ , he wouldn't have revolutionised the _____ .

4 If he hadn't got _____ , he might have become a _____ .

5 If he hadn't struck up a _____ , we wouldn't be applying his thinking to _____ .

6 If stocks are more _____ , investors should expect _____ .

7 If he hadn't made a _____ , he wouldn't have received a _____ .

8 If he hadn't spent so much time _____ , perhaps his interest in economics would have _____ .

2 Listen again and underline the main stresses in the words you added.

3 ◀》P7.04 Listen and repeat the phrases and intonation patterns.

4 Practise saying the completed sentences.

Unit 8

8.2 South African English pronunciation

1 🔊 P8.01 **Listen and tick (✓) the phrases spoken by a South African English speaker.**

1 your gut feeling ☐   **5** the go-ahead ☐

2 two weeks from now ☐   **6** all the alternatives ☐

3 hire someone to help ☐   **7** type of store ☐

4 follow your heart ☐   **8** a plan of action ☐

2 🔊 P8.02 **Listen and complete the sentences.**

1 What _____ of store would you like to _____ , and where would you want to _____ it?

2 The _____ news is that we've _____ got the _____ from the CEO.

3 Of course you have to analyse all the _____ options, but in the _____ I think it's often best to go with your initial _____ feeling.

4 Let's all get together two _____ from now, to evaluate what _____ we've made.

5 There isn't much time left, and we _____ need to settle on a plan of _____ .

6 If you don't _____ someone to help you, you'll end up having to do all the _____ yourself.

7 If you don't think through all the _____ carefully, you might end up _____ your decision.

8 When you have to make an _____ decision, do you think it's better to follow your _____ or your _____ ?

8.4 Stress and intonation in relationship-oriented decision-making

1 **Practise saying the sentences, stressing the underlined words.**

1 There's no <u>easy</u> way to say this, so I'll just <u>say</u> it.

2 Let's put it on <u>hold</u> for a few weeks.

3 How do you think we can get <u>beyond</u> this?

4 <u>Initially</u>, it looked like a good <u>idea</u>, but now I'm not so <u>sure</u>.

5 I don't want to cause any <u>hostility</u> between us.

6 To be <u>honest</u>, I have an <u>issue</u> with the lack of <u>support</u> we have for this.

7 <u>Future</u> <u>collaboration</u> is in <u>both</u> of our interests.

8 How will it <u>negatively</u> <u>affect</u> you?

9 We'd <u>both</u> like to find a <u>quick</u> <u>resolution</u> where we can keep <u>all</u> interests in <u>focus</u>.

10 We <u>both</u> have the same <u>perspective</u>.

11 We need to think about both <u>mutual</u> and <u>individual</u> gain.

12 I'd <u>like</u> to get a <u>feeling</u> for your <u>priorities</u>.

2 🔊 P8.03 **Listen and practise saying the sentences again.**

Answer key

Unit 1

Vocabulary
1 1 research   2 target
3 surveys   4 groups
5 size   6 secondary

2 1 tester   2 respondents
3 customer satisfaction
4 researchers   5 in-depth
6 analysis   7 quantitative

3 1 desk   2 gauge
3 impact   4 gather
5 launch   6 viable

Grammar
1 1 c   2 a   3 e   4 f   5 b   6 d

2 1 shall we   2 aren't they
3 do they   4 won't they
5 doesn't it   6 will we

3 1 is   2 it   3 have
4 didn't   5 has   6 isn't
7 it   8 didn't   9 aren't
10 they   11 will   12 shall

Reading
1 1 d   2 a   3 e   4 c   5 f   6 b

2 1 NG   2 F   3 T   4 T   5 NG
6 F

3 1, 4

Functional language
1 1 a   2 c   3 c   4 b
5 a   6 c   7 a

2 1 c   2 e   3 f   4 b   5 a   6 d

3 1 Sorry, we can't hear you very
well because the connection
is bad.
2 It's a bad line so let me just
repeat your question to be
sure I understood.
3 If you can email me that
question, I'll respond to
you directly.
4 This is a very delicate topic
which we need to respond
to sensitively.
5 I'm afraid that question is
outside the scope of today's
presentation.
6 Sorry, can I just stop you
there as we are pushed for
time.

Writing
1 1 demonstrated
2 half
3 respondents
4 More than
5 just
6 majority
7 participants
8 none

9 confirmed
10 the findings

2 1 e   2 d   3 b   4 a
5 g   6 c   7 f

3 **Model answer**
According to the recent
market research survey, the
new chocolate bar has not had
a positive response from our
product testers. Unfortunately,
the majority of respondents
favoured both the taste and
size of the original chocolate
bar, while almost none of the
participants preferred the new,
improved recipe. Worryingly,
almost half of those surveyed
believed that the new bar uses
cheaper ingredients, whereas
it uses premium ingredients,
increasing production costs
by 12 percent. Despite the
fact that around a third of
the responses suggested that
customers would be happy
to pay more for a better
quality product, more than
two thirds reported that they
would be unlikely to buy this
product should the current
price increase. Three quarters
of the testers also raised
concerns that the quality does
not reflect the luxury brand
image. Interestingly, despite
the negative comments about
the taste of the product, the
findings also indicated that
a quarter of the participants
would be interested in seeing
more flavours added to the
current range. The survey
confirmed that we need to
reconsider both the improved
recipe and the pricing of
the product. As a result,
we will carry out further
improvements and a further
round of market research
before launching the product.

4 b

Unit 2

Vocabulary
1 1 nurturing
2 isolated
3 mentoring
4 candid
5 feedback
6 peers
7 benefits
8 compassionate

2 1 cooperative
2 two-way
3 beneficial
4 interests, heart
5 call, shots
6 inclusion

Grammar
1 1 b   2 c   3 a   4 c   5 b   6 a

2 1 The thing, Something
2 will be, is
3 what, something
4 The thing, What
5 was, wasn't
6 Things, The things

3 1 The things that we cannot
compromise on are quality
and reliability.
2 What one successful
business did was to allow
employees to work from
home.
3 The areas of business that
most interest graduates are
finance or consultancy.
4 What I will do is make sure
that the work is completed
before the deadline.
5 It was a technological
problem that was the cause
of the delay, not our staff.
6 Something that works for us
is having regular meetings
to update the team.

Listening
1 1 g   2 b   3 d   4 c   5 e

2 1 emotional
2 workplace
3 managers
4 appropriately
5 relationships
6 empathy
7 understanding
8 managing

3 1 F   2 T   3 T   4 T

Functional language
1 1 e   2 d   3 a   4 f   5 b   6 c

2 1 open, up
2 check, page
3 both, issues
4 to, second
5 best, tackle
6 benefits, thinking

3 1 b   2 c   3 b

Writing
1 … where we require
improvements in team
performance for [**the**]
next project.

Firstly, we [**would**] like you to schedule … As project leader, you need [**to**] check progress and communicate any concerns to your manager [**so**] that problems can be solved …

… face-to-face meetings with the client [**at**] the start of the project … regular calls to [**find**] out if they require

… arrange for a member of your team to prepare [**an**] online survey after each project is complete [**in**] order to check customer satisfaction. Arrange follow [**up**] calls for customers … Speak to the HR manager next week [**for**] more information …

2 **Model answer**
Dear Maria,

We are delighted that you have completed the first part of our training course and passed your exams with distinction. You are now ready to move on to the next part of your training. As we discussed in our meeting yesterday, there are some areas where improvements are required for the next part of your course.

Firstly, you will need to attend seminars and lectures more regularly so that you do not miss course content. If you are not able to get to the class, we expect you to let the lecturer know as soon as possible.

Secondly, it is important that you spend more time preparing for projects. Your written reports are good but they do need to include more research. I would also like to stress how important it is to hand the assignments in on time. Last term, some of your essays and project work were late and therefore you lost marks in your end-of-term result.

Finally, we would like you to arrange weekly face-to-face meetings with your tutor. This is in order to discuss your progress and so that she can help you with planning and with any parts of the course you may be finding difficult. Previous candidates have found this enormously helpful.

You have made a good start on the training course and we

look forward to watching your progress in the next term.

Yours sincerely,

3 c

Unit 3
Vocabulary
1 1 withdrawn 2 financial
3 prohibitive 4 banking
5 transfer 6 payee
7 accounting 8 deposits
2 1 fee 2 bill
3 money order 4 debit card
5 rent 6 direct debit
7 cheque 8 savings

Grammar
1 1 by 2 out 3 by
4 up 5 with 6 forward
2 1 a 2 a & b 3 b
4 b 5 a & b 6 a
3 **a** 2, 5 **b** 1 **c** 3, 4, 6

Reading
1 1 g 2 b 3 f 4 d
5 a 6 h 7 e
2 1 M 2 F 3 M
4 M 5 F 6 F
3 1, 4

Functional language
1 1 d 2 h 3 a 4 g
5 b 6 e 7 f 8 c
2 1 These are the reasons which warrant
2 when we considered the big picture
3 If we fail to act, then
4 The consequence of that would be
5 can see why there might be objections
6 this idea is the best opportunity
3 1 action, mean C
2 break down, reasons D
3 idea, opportunity D
4 should, current C
5 achieve, target C
6 backing, others D

Writing
1 1 c 2 f 3 e 4 b
5 d 6 h 7 a 8 g
2 **Model answer**
Dear Sir/Madam,

We are writing to express our dissatisfaction with your service. Ten weeks ago, we ordered 2,000 personalised

key rings to give to visitors attending a conference. We gave notice that this was a large order and that these items would need to be personalised with our company logo. We also agreed a 12 percent discount due to the size of the order.

Having informed you well in advance of our requirements and receiving written confirmation that everything was in order, we did not anticipate any issues. However, we were informed on Monday that you will now only be able to supply 75 percent of the order with logos. Also, the price quoted on your letter does not include any discount. We have called your customer services department but received no response. We feel that you have dealt with this matter most unprofessionally. Your actions have damaged both our plans for the conference and also our trust in your company.

As a potential regular customer, we request that you kindly resolve this matter immediately and also increase the discount to 25 percent to reflect the key rings which will now be supplied without a logo. Unless you do this, we shall be forced to find another supplier for all future contracts.

We look forward to your prompt response.

Yours faithfully,

3 b

Unit 4
Vocabulary
1 1 threat
2 weather
3 temperatures
4 change
5 atmosphere
6 demand
7 environment
8 difficulties
2 1 extreme weather
2 pose a threat
3 high temperatures
4 humid atmosphere
5 face difficulties
6 unstable environment

3 1 production 2 predict
  3 embrace 4 protect
  5 sustainable 6 potential

Grammar

1 1 had become
  2 will have become
  3 has/have used
  4 will have used
  5 has/have forgotten
  6 had forgotten
  7 had lived
  8 will have lived

2 1 b 2 a 3 c 4 b 5 c

3 1 will have advanced
  2 correct
  3 hadn't tested
  4 will have experienced
  5 correct
  6 will have installed
  7 correct
  8 has increased

Listening

1 1 T 2 F 3 F 4 T
  5 F 6 T 7 T 8 F

2 1 costs
  2 cyberattacks
  3 hacking
  4 network
  5 data
  6 threats
  7 damage
  8 analyse
  9 identify
  10 systems
  11 improvements
  12 stage

3 1 A 2 N 3 T 4 N

Functional language

1 1 b 2 a 3 b 4 a 5 a

2 a 2,3 b 1,5 c 6

3 1 matter 2 point
  3 objectively 4 overlooking
  5 elaborate 6 unreasonable
  7 benefits 8 correctly

4 **A:** I heard that you were upset about not being selected to lead the project?
  B: That's right. Could you elaborate on why I wasn't considered suitable?
  A: I understand that you're disappointed, but can we look at this objectively for a moment? You haven't yet developed the management skills a role like this requires.
  B: Are you perhaps overlooking the fact that I managed teams in my previous position?

A: I get your point, but this is a very different type of team. It would be useful for you to have further leadership training to help you enter into the role confidently.
B: OK, I can see the benefits of what you're saying. And if I follow you correctly, you mean that if I agree to additional training, you'll consider me ready to lead a project?
A: The fact of the matter is that we would need to see how the training goes. After the course we could discuss potential projects that might be a good fit for you.
B: That doesn't sound unreasonable. Can we discuss some logical next steps?
A: Do you mean in terms of arranging the course? Sure. Come and speak to me tomorrow and we'll look at the best way to proceed.

Writing

1 1 courses 2 options
  3 approach 4 investigate
  5 recommend 6 advisable
  7 into 8 Consequently

2 **Model answer**
Taking all the factors mentioned into account, there are two courses of action to improve time management. There were many suggestions made, which included hiring a consultant on a temporary contract or using the HR department. Having considered the options, a reasonable approach would seem to be to use a team from HR to carry out initial research. This would take place in three steps and would include the following: investigating the effectiveness of our current work patterns and conducting consultations with all staff to discover any issues which employees feel might affect task efficiency in their role. As the third step, we will investigate ways to improve staff engagement, for example, by providing suggestion boxes or running competitions for the best idea to improve productivity. Some of the recent problems we have experienced have

occurred as a result of sudden changes made to work rotas. Because these were made without giving staff sufficient advance warning, there were a significant number of complaints. Therefore, I would also like to recommend new procedures which would allow at least three days' notice for any changes to rotas. It would also be advisable to use online tools to manage projects so that everyone has access to the schedules at any given time. Finally, I propose we carry out additional training on time management for all employees over the next three weeks.

3 c

Unit 5

Vocabulary

1 1 developmental
  2 international
  3 perspective
  4 brief
  5 mobility
  6 settle
  7 claim
  8 deposit

2 1 assignment 2 mobilised
  3 shipment 4 adoption
  5 taxable 6 compensatory

3 **Across:**
  1 immigrant 3 compensate
  4 assign 6 process
  7 relocation 8 mobility
  Down:
  2 globalisation 5 ship

Grammar

1 1 a, c 2 b, c 3 a, b
  4 a, c 5 b, c

2 1 should 2 have 3 did
  4 are 5 will 6 had

3 1 Not until she received the letter did she believe she had won first place.
  2 Only if we are given more information can we make a decision.
  3 Little did we know that property prices were about to fall.
  4 Under no circumstances would we consider this to be an acceptable offer.
  5 Not once did they give him any feedback on his performance.
  6 Only by finding a compromise can we guarantee job security.

7 Seldom have we heard such a convincing presentation.

8 Not only did he get an interview, but they also offered him the job.

Listening

1 family, mentor support, loneliness, cultural issues

2 **1** c **2** b **3** c **4** b
5 b **6** c **7** a

3 **1** link **2** vital
3 fail **4** personal
5 effect **6** financial
7 avoid

Functional language

1 **1** rewarding **2** evidence
3 demonstrate **4** respond
5 excelled **6** follow
7 a tendency **8** room
9 improve **10** thoughts
11 achieved

2 **1** One clear benefit
2 The obvious thing to do
3 don't take this opportunity
4 In a nutshell
5 the worst
6 a matter of talking
7 the twin benefits

3 **a** 2, 6 **b** 1 **c** 7 **d** 4 **e** 3 **f** 5

Writing

1 **1** Thanks **2** highly
3 beneficial **4** downside
5 understanding **6** exchange
7 expectations **8** Although

2 Background information: 2
Sequence of events: 1, 3, 6, 8, 12
Pros and cons: 4, 5, 7, 9, 10
Conclusion: 11

3 **Model answer**
Hello from Shanghai!

Well, here I finally am in Shanghai thanks to the company secondment programme. It was quite a culture shock when I got off the plane, but I'm very excited to be here. I arrived last week and was met by Chao, from the office, who spoke very good English.

He introduced me to my manager, Mr Huang. Chao then took me to the company apartment where I'll be staying. It's quite small, but it has everything I need. I started work the next morning and was shown my desk in a huge open-plan office. Mr Huang introduced me to most of the staff during the day.

The work is very interesting and it's giving me a better global perspective. I'm also learning to adapt to the different work culture. At first, I thought my colleagues didn't like me, but I've discovered it's because they are worried about their English – they shouldn't be as it's really very good!

The main downsides are that I don't speak Mandarin very well and the working hours are longer than at home.

However, I'm really looking forward to improving my Mandarin and learning all about the local culture and history. I am sure that this experience will be beneficial to my career progression and I highly recommend it to everyone.

4 a

Unit 6

Vocabulary

1 **1** strategic **2** gain
3 access **4** presence
5 win-win **6** outweighed
7 stake **8** regulatory

2 **1** shareholders **2** joint venture
3 takeover **4** synergy
5 acquisition

3 **1** share **2** resources
3 benefit **4** foundation
5 turnaround

Grammar

1 **1** should / ought to
2 could / ought to
3 couldn't
4 shouldn't
5 couldn't / can't
6 may

2 **1** She couldn't have expected the project to run smoothly with such an inexperienced team.
2 We ought to have discussed the merger before any decisions were made.
3 He can't have lost his phone because he's just called me from the airport.
4 They shouldn't have signed the contract without consulting their lawyer first.
5 You might have forgotten to make a note of the deadline in your diary.
6 Their previous appointment must have run late as we were due to start this meeting ten minutes ago.

3 **1** might have found
2 couldn't have written
3 must have agreed
4 can't have gone
5 may have decided
6 should have responded

Reading

1 **1** F **2** B **3** C **4** E **5** D

2 **1** markets **2** revenue
3 base **4** collaborative
5 differences **6** trust
7 goals **8** procedures
9 confidential

3 b

Functional language

1 **1** straight to the point
2 most concerns me
3 if we were to
4 you be prepared
5 potential problem
6 let's figure out
7 I'll agree to set up
8 to raise the issues
9 reach a compromise

2 **1** ways **2** meant
3 hindsight **4** expected
5 foreseen **6** takeaway
7 in **8** Considering
9 forward

Writing

1 **1** hope **2** discussion
3 lack **4** failure
5 clear **6** result

2 **1** in the hope of expanding
2 is hardly any advantage
3 is evident (that) there is
4 these reasons
5 does not appear to be

3 **Model answer**
We have been awarded a new contract to build 2,000 homes over the next two years, and due to the size of the project and the need to complete it on time, we have been in discussions with our main supplier about the possibility of a strategic alliance. Currently, we are very close to reaching an agreement regarding all the details of the contract and our shared strategy.

We made the decision in the hope of both growing the business and ensuring a smooth supply chain for all the required materials for this project. Supply of materials has been a huge issue on our last two projects, where several important deadlines were missed due to delayed deliveries of key materials. With the delivery times guaranteed from our alliance partner, we would be able to avoid a repeat of the same mistakes. Both companies have the same objectives and are looking to expand. Furthermore, we are keen to share our skills, knowledge and expertise to benefit both companies.

It is evident that a close working relationship can only be beneficial to both companies and we look forward to working on even more large projects in the future. However, we are fully aware that we would need to have clear lines of communication and that procedures and job roles would need to be very clearly defined.

4 a, d, f

Unit 7

Vocabulary

1 **1** thinking **2** pose
3 measures **4** suffered
5 mitigated **6** solutions
7 stock **8** disaster

2 **Across:**
4 are **6** potential
7 reduce
Down:
1 take **2** minimise
3 calculated **5** major

3 **1** analysis **2** hazards
3 manage **4** prevent
5 run

Grammar

1 **a** 2,8 **b** 1,5 **c** 3,6 **d** 4,7
2 **1** c **2** b **3** a **4** b **5** a **6** c
3 **1** ~~would~~ **wouldn't**
2 ~~weren't~~ **wouldn't be**
3 ~~didn't crash~~ **hadn't crashed**
4 ~~would be~~ **were / had been**
5 ~~doesn't~~ **wouldn't**

Listening

1 **a** 3 **b** 1 **c** 5 **d** 2 **e** 4
2 **1** predict
2 volatile
3 inflation
4 negative effect
5 assets
6 strong returns
7 fund managers
8 technology
9 economic recovery
10 safety net
11 spending

12 emotion
13 stocks
14 top
3 c

Functional language

1 **1** for **2** case
3 time **4** expect
5 give **6** arise
7 overcautious **8** cover
2 **1** probability **2** methods
3 cause **4** an urgent
5 identified **6** radar
3 **a** 2,6 **b** 5 **c** 1,3 **d** 4

Writing

1 **1** involved **2** Date
3 details **4** Injuries
5 Analysis **6** Causes
7 Recommendations
8 How to avoid
2 **1** was injured
2 was lifting
3 hurt
4 was checked
5 will not be
6 have just filled
7 will find
8 to remind
3 **Model answer**

Facts	
Person(s) involved	Jack Roberts, metal worker
Date, time and location	7th July at 11.30 a.m. Engineering plant A
Full details of incident	Jack was working on one of our new engines when he turned round to get something from the work bench behind him. However, he did not see a piece of equipment which had been left on the floor by another employee and he tripped over it, hitting his head on the bench.
Injuries and treatment	When Jack fell, he twisted his ankle and also hit and cut his head on the work bench. The company nurse checked his ankle, which had started to swell up quite badly. She recommended that he went immediately to hospital for an X-ray. Before he went, she cleaned up the cut on his head.

Analysis	
Causes of incident	There seems to be one main reason for this accident: the fact that another employee had left some equipment on the floor. This is against health and safety regulations .

Recommendations	
How to avoid it in future	It is clear that all staff need to be reminded of the dangers of leaving equipment unattended around the plant. I recommend that they receive more training on all aspects of the health and safety rules.

Unit 8

Vocabulary

1 **1** driving **2** collected
3 examined **4** identify
5 reconsidered **6** given
7 monitor
2 **1** making **2** forward
3 gut **4** pulling
5 ending **6** settle
7 alternative
3 **1** evaluate **2** implemented
3 consider **4** defined
5 criteria **6** constraints
7 developed

Grammar

1 **1** making **2** to hold
3 discussing **4** to consider
5 to speak **6** keeping
2 **1** taking **2** coming
3 to do **4** to make
5 to survive **6** having
7 to think **8** not making
9 weighing **10** creating
3 **1** a **2** a **3** b **4** a
5 b **6** b **7** a **8** a

Reading

1 **1** D **2** C **3** A **4** E **5** B
2 **1** T **2** F **3** T **4** F **5** T
6 F **7** T
3 c

Functional language

1 **1** of the matter
2 lack of
3 personally
4 our feelings
5 cloud
6 instinct would be
7 true that

8 black and white
9 even though

2 1 had   2 way
   3 where   4 like
   5 between   6 get
   7 interests   8 issue
   9 feeling   10 hold

Writing

1 1 enable   2 be improved
   3 assure   4 guarantee
   5 view   6 consider

2 b

3 **Model answer**

Dear Mr Champeau,

Further to our discussions last week, we have decided to set up a new Sales and Marketing office in Rome. The Italian market is growing fast and currently it is serviced by your office in Paris. This means that we are unable to take advantage of this growth in the way we would like and that customers often find it difficult to contact the Sales Manager if they have any problems.

The office in Rome will enable us to have a much closer relationship with our Italian clients. It is important to have a presence in the country so we can have face-to-face contact with individual customers. It will also allow us to work on expanding our market share in that region.

We realise that there may be a period of readjustment in the Paris office but we can assure you that no one will be made redundant as we are hoping to expand our market share in that area, too.

In view of this, we are offering a six-month secondment for two staff members from the Paris office to oversee setting up the Rome office. Please let me know which of your staff may be interested and who you would recommend. A knowledge of Italian would be helpful, but knowledge and experience of our company are more important.

Yours sincerely,

Gareth Higham
Sales & Marketing Director

Pronunciation

Unit 1

1.2

1 Checking: 1, 2, 5, 6, 7
Asking: 3, 4, 8

3 1 shouldn't they
   2 wouldn't you
   3 is there
   4 doesn't it
   5 shouldn't they
   6 doesn't it
   7 shall we
   8 aren't we

1.3

1 1, 4, 5, 7, 8

2 1 It's not something we have time to look at today.
   2 I'm not entirely sure of the answer to that question.
   3 I'll respond directly to you. Is that OK?
   4 That question is outside the scope of today's presentation.
   5 We need to be mindful that many people feel very strongly about this.
   6 We covered that at the beginning of the presentation when I talked about …
   7 What's the main question you have on this?
   8 You'd be better off asking my colleague in Finance about this issue.

Unit 2

2.2

1 1 What I'll do <u>tomorrow</u> (**fall-rise**) is to make sure the <u>contract</u> (**fall**) is <u>ready</u>.
   2 It was the boring <u>work</u> (**fall**) that made him <u>leave</u>.
   3 Something they forgot to <u>take</u> (**fall-rise**) was the latest version of the <u>agreement</u> (**fall**).
   4 What we'll have to <u>rethink</u> (**fall-rise**) are our <u>conditions</u> of <u>employment</u> (**fall**).
   5 It's the supplier in <u>Mexico</u> (**fall**) that my boss is trying to reach.
   6 The innovation that <u>didn't</u> (**fall-rise**) work was the one that was most <u>expensive</u> (**fall**).

3 1 **B:** It's my <u>boss</u> (**fall**) that's trying to get through to them.
   2 **B:** It's the <u>manufacturer</u> (**fall**) in Mexico I'm trying to reach.
   3 **B:** What they <u>criticised</u> (**fall-rise**) was the lack of <u>time</u> (**fall**) to implement them.
   4 **B:** What made him <u>leave</u> (**fall-rise**) was the boring <u>work</u> (**fall**) he had to do.
   5 **B:** What made <u>me</u> (**fall-rise**) leave was the <u>atmosphere</u> (**fall**) in the office.
   6 **B:** Unfortunately the only one they <u>forgot</u> (**fall-rise**) to take was the <u>latest</u> (**fall**) one.

2.4

1 1, 2, 4, 5, 6, 8

2 1 Do you see any quick wins here?
   2 I think both perspectives are very valid.
   3 Let me make sure we all understood what you said.
   4 Any reflections from your side?
   5 We don't really see eye to eye on this.
   6 You can see from the agenda what we're all looking to achieve today.
   7 We need to increase the insurance for the project.
   8 What's your take on this, Jack?

Unit 3

3.2

1 1 She <u>carried on</u> living with her mother.
   2 She managed to <u>put</u> some money <u>by</u> each month.
   3 She wanted to <u>save up</u> before studying at university.
   4 She didn't want to <u>fall behind</u> with the rent.
   5 Her grandfather had <u>set up</u> a trust fund for her.

3 1 He set a <u>trust fund</u> up.
   2 He <u>set</u> it <u>up</u>.
   3 She wanted to <u>save</u> some <u>money</u> up.
   4 The problem has <u>come up</u> before.
   5 What if your <u>computer</u> breaks down?
   6 He wouldn't be <u>able</u> to <u>pay</u> them <u>back</u>.
   7 They <u>agreed</u> to pay <u>off</u> his <u>debts</u>.
   8 They <u>agreed</u> to pay them <u>off</u>.

3.3

1 <u>Then</u> … / <u>try</u> and <u>visualise</u> / the <u>looks</u> on your <u>guests'</u> <u>faces</u> / as they <u>enter</u> the <u>ballroom</u> / and <u>see</u> more than <u>one hundred circus</u> performers / <u>all</u> dressed in <u>gold</u>. / <u>Fire</u> acts! / <u>Acrobats</u>! / <u>Jugglers</u>! / <u>Trapeze</u> artists! / <u>All</u> <u>surrounded</u> by <u>enormous</u> golden <u>urns</u> / with <u>thousands</u> of <u>flowers</u> / <u>cascading</u> <u>from</u> them. / <u>Imagine</u> how <u>everyone</u> will <u>react</u> / to this <u>incredible</u> <u>sight</u>.

Unit 4

4.2

1 **1** How many computers had been affected?
2 They still haven't recovered.
3 The ransomware had been aimed at banks.
4 He said he'd been told.
5 They'd chosen their targets carefully.
6 A UK plant will have been targeted.

3 **1** Before I worked in this office, I'd never worked at a smart desk.
2 The virus has spread quickly.
3 I've never seen this kind of smart building before.
4 By the time I'd installed it, it was out of date.
5 I've worked for the company for nearly two years.
6 They thought they hadn't been hit, but they had, in fact.
7 They still haven't brought the system back online.
8 They hadn't chosen random targets.
9 I'm sure they'll have been able to respond.
10 I don't think we've been affected, have we?
11 By the end of the day we'll have been given all the details.
12 They thought they'd escaped, but they haven't.

Unit 5

5.1

1

Oo	culture process processed shipping
oO	assign assigned employ
Ooo	cultural globalised immigrant mobilise taxable

oOo	adopted assignment seconded taxation
ooO	employee relocate
ooOo	immigration relocated
ooOoo	compensatory
oooOo	globalisation

3 **1** accommodation oooOo
2 helpful Oo
3 personal Ooo
4 development oOoo
5 compensation ooOo
6 interpreter oOoo
7 opportunities ooOoo
8 permanently Oooo
9 organisation oooOo

5.2

1 **1** Rarely does anyone I know get any really exciting opportunities.
2 Little did I know how difficult it would be to learn a new language.
3 Never in my life have I been treated so badly by an employer.
4 Not only was the work interesting, but I also got to know something of a different culture.
5 At no time was she offered any kind of support.
6 No sooner had she arrived than she knew she'd be happy there.
7 In no way am I saying that you were responsible for what happened.
8 On no account should you sign the contract in its present form.
9 Only much later did I realise what a great experience it had been.
10 Not only did they have to book a flight, but they also had to find accommodation.
11 Not until he began the job did he realise it was the opportunity of a lifetime.
12 Under no circumstances would I accept that assignment abroad.

Unit 6

6.2

1 **1** They must have been working late.
2 You oughtn't to have left the company.
3 They couldn't have left on time.

4 You should take the other job.
5 They can't have known that the brand would become so popular.

3 **1** Don't you think we should have joined forces?
2 We obviously couldn't have predicted what the results of the merger would be.
3 They could really have kept the brand name, couldn't they?
4 There might have been a lot of different possibilities.
5 They may have wanted to make use of synergy.
6 Shouldn't you have left earlier to be on time for your appointment?
7 The company could actually have grown faster under different ownership.
8 A strategic alliance might perhaps have been a good idea.
9 Couldn't you have taken on the new role you were offered?
10 They can't possibly have told you the details, because they don't know them themselves yet.
11 They must have been trying to decrease competition, mustn't they?
12 They say we should have solved the problem months ago, but I can't see how we could have.

6.4

1 1, 2, 4, 6, 8

2 **1** Considering everything that happened I'm very proud of what we achieved.
2 In future, roles and responsibilities should be defined more clearly.
3 My main lesson learnt is that problems need to be addressed early.
4 With hindsight, we should have used a project planning tool.
5 One thing I hadn't expected was that they'd need so much guidance.
6 What are your thoughts on this?
7 In many ways, I think that the main problem was a leadership failure.
8 This created the problem that people had different versions of the schedule.

Unit 7

7.1

1
1 /w/   2 /r/   3 /w/
4 /w/   5 /r/   6 /r/
7 /r/   8 /r/

3
1 Keep the weight‿of the building‿as light‿as possible.
2 Many buildings have to be demolished‿after‿ earthquakes.
3 Buildings‿in the capital‿are more‿at risk than those‿in‿ other‿areas.
4 How do‿earthquakes‿affect business‿and the economy?
5 Have you‿ever worked‿in‿a skyscraper?
6 Fire‿alarms‿are‿an‿effective means‿of saving lives.
7 Smart systems‿ automatically reduce risk to people‿in‿a building.
8 The lifts stop‿automatically at the nearest floor.

4
1 Keep the weight‿of the building‿as light‿as possible.
2 Many buildings have to be demolished‿after /r/ earthquakes.
3 Buildings‿in the capital‿are more /r/ at risk than those‿ in‿other /r/ areas.
4 How do /w/ earthquakes‿ affect business‿and the economy?
5 Have you /w/ ever worked‿ in‿a skyscraper?
6 Fire /r/ alarms‿are /r/ an‿ effective means‿of saving lives.
7 Smart systems‿ automatically reduce risk to people‿in‿a building.
8 The lifts stop‿automatically at the nearest floor.

7.2

1
1 If he were a teenager today, he probably wouldn't have spent his early childhood playing the violin.
2 If he hadn't decided to pursue a graduate degree in economics, he wouldn't have gravitated towards uncertainty.
3 If it hadn't been for a chance meeting, he wouldn't have revolutionised the investment industry.
4 If he hadn't got interested in economics, he might have become a great violinist.
5 If he hadn't struck up a conversation with a stockbroker, we wouldn't be applying his thinking to markets today.
6 If stocks are more volatile than bonds, investors should expect better returns.
7 If he hadn't made a key contribution to economics, he wouldn't have received a Nobel Prize.
8 If he hadn't spent so much time playing baseball, perhaps his interest in economics would have developed earlier.

2
1 If he were a teenager <u>today</u>, he probably wouldn't have spent his early childhood playing the <u>violin</u>.
2 If he hadn't decided to pursue a graduate degree in <u>economics</u>, he wouldn't have gravitated towards <u>uncertainty</u>.
3 If it hadn't been for a chance <u>meeting</u>, he wouldn't have revolutionised the <u>investment</u> industry.
4 If he hadn't got interested in <u>economics</u>, he might have become a great <u>violinist</u>.
5 If he hadn't struck up a conversation with a <u>stockbroker</u>, we wouldn't be applying his thinking to markets <u>today</u>.
6 If stocks are more volatile than <u>bonds</u>, investors should expect better <u>returns</u>.
7 If he hadn't made a key contribution to <u>economics</u>, he wouldn't have received a Nobel <u>Prize</u>.
8 If he hadn't spent so much time playing <u>baseball</u>, perhaps his interest in economics would have developed <u>earlier</u>.

Unit 8

8.2

1 2, 3, 5, 6, 8

2
1 What type of store would you like to open, and where would you want to locate it?
2 The good news is that we've finally got the go-ahead from the CEO.
3 Of course you have to analyse all the different options, but in the end I think it's often best to go with your initial gut feeling.
4 Let's all get together two weeks from now, to evaluate what progress we've made.
5 There isn't much time left, and we urgently need to settle on a plan of action.
6 If you don't hire someone to help you, you'll end up having to do all the work yourself.
7 If you don't think through all the alternatives carefully, you might end up regretting your decision.
8 When you have to make an important decision, do you think it's better to follow your heart or your head?

2.01

E = Ethan   M = Mia

E: Welcome to WorkHacks, the podcast that explores how ideas from the world of psychology can be used in the workplace. I'm your host Ethan Marks and today we are speaking to Mia Newton, HR Director and Trainer.
Thanks for coming in, Mia. Now you wanted to talk to us about the importance of emotional intelligence for managers, is that right?

M: Thanks for inviting me, Ethan. Yes, we often hear about the importance of emotional intelligence in the workplace. But I want to focus on how it can be of use in creating positive working relationships between management and employees.

E: So, let's start at the beginning. What exactly is emotional intelligence?

M: Well, it's a combination of understanding and managing your own emotions as well as those of others. So, it's about expressing emotions appropriately and also handling interpersonal relationships effectively. Just because we are in a professional or work situation doesn't mean that our emotions are turned off. We can still feel stress or annoyance or have to deal with people who are worried, upset or angry.

E: Can you give us a practical example?

M: Yes, a manager that I worked with recently had an employee who returned to work after a long illness. What the manager did was to ask one of her colleagues to help by taking on some of the bigger projects. He was trying to make sure that her first few weeks back at work weren't too stressful.

E: And did that work?

M: No, it went very badly. It became obvious that the returning member of staff was unhappy and her colleague, who was doing some of her work, was stressed. Communication between the two colleagues became very difficult. What the manager failed to do was to think about how the two members of staff might feel about this idea before putting the plans into action. After he spoke to them both he realized that the employee returning to work felt that he didn't trust her to do her job. At the same time, her colleague was stressed because he had extra projects to do in addition to his normal work. It didn't work for either person.

E: So, it was a communication breakdown that caused the problem?

M: I believe that the problem with communication was an effect not the cause. The real cause was that the manager didn't use emotional intelligence. He didn't stop and think about how his team members might feel about the changes he made. He acted with kindness, but he didn't use empathy which would mean understanding how his actions might make them feel.

E: Tell us a bit more about empathy – is it the same as sympathy? And why is it important?

M: Well, sympathy means feeling pity or compassion for someone. So, for example, the manager I mentioned felt sympathy for his employee who was coming back to work after being ill and he wanted to make things easier for her return. Empathy, on the other hand, is much more about putting yourself in someone else's shoes – you know, trying to gain a sense of what they are feeling and experiencing and understanding why.

E: So, in the situation with the manager, what difference would empathy have made?

M: Well, for a start the manager was looking at this mainly as a practical problem. How to deal with the workload for the employee's return. He could sympathize and didn't want her first weeks back at work to be stressful. But he didn't consider how taking away projects might make her feel or how it might impact her colleague. So, the first step would have been to talk to both members of staff individually to discuss the idea and see how they felt. If he had done this, he would have learned that his employee was looking forward to the challenge of coming back to work and she was excited by the projects, so when some of these were taken away and given to a colleague, she felt demotivated.

E: Don't you think that all this talk of emotions, emotional intelligence and empathy is going to be difficult for some managers?

M: Like all tools for the workplace, it's about understanding why it is useful and how to use it. It's actually very practical and isn't all about sitting around talking about feelings. Managers sometimes have to make hard calls. They may need to make difficult decisions about their workforce, give difficult feedback or fire people. But it is still possible to carry out these actions with empathy, which will ultimately lead to a better outcome. The role is about being a manager of people and emotional intelligence is about managing emotions. These two skills work well together.

E: All very interesting, thanks, Mia. We have to stop there for today but Mia will be with us again next time to look at the key steps that help managers use emotional intelligence effectively with their team.

 4.01

T = Tom   A = Angela

T: Good morning, Angela. I'm Tom Winterson from Aztec Cyber Security Consultants. Thanks for inviting me in today.

A: Thanks for coming, Tom. We appreciate having your expert advice. As you know, FairWay is an online retailer selling golfing products and we've had reports that a number of similar organisations have experienced cyberattacks recently. This is obviously of concern to us because we need to make sure that our customers' data is secure.

T: That's understandable, Angela. We're aware that a number of similar online businesses have recently experienced challenges to their security systems either through hacking of customers' personal information or by a direct attack on the company's computer network – and that this has disrupted sales.

A: That's right. But am I correct in thinking that the main issue is that these organisations were using outdated security software? We've recently updated the software on our computer network and we haven't had any security problems so far. Can I assume our system is pretty secure now?

T: Unfortunately, it isn't as simple as that, Angela. Cyberattackers are becoming increasingly sophisticated which means that even companies with up-to-date systems such as yours have had their online ordering systems targeted. As a result, the organisations affected weren't able to carry out sales transactions because their online ordering systems had come to a standstill.

A: That's what we absolutely want to avoid. Something like that could do significant damage to our brand and destroy the trust of our clients.

T: Exactly, that's why it is vital not to become complacent. The challenge for online retailers is that the security threats are constantly changing.

A: So, what do you suggest? If I've understood you correctly, it would be impossible to create a system that's completely safe from attack.

T: That's true. So, as a first step, it would be a good idea for us to analyse the types of cyberattacks taking place at the moment, and identify which could potentially pose the greatest threat to you.

A: How exactly will that help us if the threats keep changing?

T: You're right that no system can be completely safe from attack but the analysis stage will help us categorise those risks into immediate, medium-term and long-term. Also, we use the information to make accurate predictions about which might cause the most damage to your particular system and that allows us to minimise the risk for your company both now and in the future.

A: Ah, OK, that sounds useful. And how would you proceed after that?

T: After the analysis stage, I'd take a close look at your current systems to see where any improvements could be recommended.

A: Can you give me an idea of how long that would take? We're obviously keen to move ahead with this as soon as possible.

T: Of course, if you could introduce me to your IT team, I can speak to them about some safety procedures that you could use immediately. I could then get back to you with the analysis and recommendations by the end of the week. How does that sound?

A: That's great. Can you give me an estimate of how much this would cost? We're a relatively new business and we don't have a huge budget like some of our larger competitors.

T: Certainly. After I've spoken to IT, I'll have a clearer idea how much work is involved. I'll drop you an email with an accurate idea of prices for each stage.

A: That sounds perfect, thanks Tom.

🔊 5.01

I = Interviewer   A = Alyn

I: Welcome to Business Matters, the weekly podcast for managers. Today we're talking to Alyn Mitchell, an expert on relocation and what it means for companies trying to retain their staff during this time. Welcome Alyn. Now, we all know how difficult it can be to retain our best staff during a relocation, so can you explain how companies can achieve this?

A: Well, first of all, I need to make it clear that at this point I'm not talking about relocating the whole company to another geographic location, along with most of its staff. That's much more difficult and many staff members will likely be unwilling to relocate. Today, I'm only going to focus on the deployment of key individuals who will work in another country for anything from six months up to two years. Although seconding key individuals should be easier, if not handled properly, the relocation can go badly wrong and could lead to a valuable employee leaving the company altogether.

I: Does seconding individuals like this happen quite often, then?

A: Yes, very, in fact. In today's global environment, it's more common than ever and companies need to get it right.

I: But I would have thought that the opportunity to live and work in another country would be very attractive to most people.

A: It's true that it is many people's dream, but it isn't everyone's. However, those who do volunteer to go sometimes have problems which they didn't anticipate. That's why it's important for companies to understand this and ensure that mobility teams are there to help the employee to get the most out of the experience. The more a company knows about the employee, the better.

I: What do you mean, exactly?

A: It's not until we consider the move from the employee's point of view that we can understand why some organisations lose talent, simply because a relocation has been badly handled. That's where retention comes in. If a company wishes to keep key employees on board then it needs to deal with the move sensitively.

I: So, what are some of the key things a company should consider when relocating staff?

A: Firstly, it needs to find out whether the employee would be moving with a partner or family and how the move would impact each of them. Many relocations have failed because the employee and his or her family weren't well enough prepared.

I: Yes, I can imagine.

A: For example, there's the story of someone who returned after only a month because his family couldn't find their favourite take-out food in the new country. It sounds unbelievable, really, but if the company had prepared the family properly, they would have known this before agreeing to go. And apart from the obvious things like weather, food and language, there are often big cultural differences that need to be addressed, too. Living in another country requires a certain amount of flexibility from everyone involved.

I: Isn't it expensive for a company to prepare partners and families for the move?

A: It can be, but if you're talking about a valuable employee, then the expense is worth it. But if an employee relocates with a partner or family and returns home very quickly, it will have been a huge waste of money for the company. It should never underestimate the importance of the people closest to that employee.

I: So, wouldn't it therefore be better to send only single people, you know, those without any close ties at home?

A: No, not at all. Companies should always send the best person for the job and if an employee's usual support network is strong and moves with them, then they can overcome difficulties together and it can be a positive experience for everyone. Moreover, people who relocate alone have often found it difficult to integrate and they end up feeling quite isolated and lonely. In an ideal world, the employee should feel able to discuss these issues with HR but sometimes they might see it as a failure on their part. As a result, the employee becomes more isolated and disaffected with their position. It can become a vicious circle.

I: So, a good secondment can help a company retain their best staff but a poorly managed one can achieve quite the opposite.

A: Exactly. It's all about preparation and good communication from the company's perspective. It needs to understand all issues and have a strategy in place to deal with them before the individual is relocated. Then it must implement a good support policy for the employee who has been relocated, for example, by providing them with a buddy or mentor to help them when they arrive. And it's crucially important to get feedback while the employee is there and as soon as they return in order to address any issues which may arise.

🔊 7.01

Speaker 1: All investments carry an element of risk because unfortunately, nobody can accurately predict which sectors are going to perform best. Everyone has a particular favourite but it's wise to keep looking for something different. In my view, you can't go far wrong investing in gold. It's a good diversifier because it doesn't perform well when the outlook is positive and markets are going upwards, but it does come into its own when investors are wary and markets are more volatile. They turn to gold when they're looking to protect their capital from falling markets. In addition, the long-term performance of gold has proved to be good at protecting against inflation.

Speaker 2: If you invest too much money in one area that underperforms, then this can have a significant negative effect on your overall finances. Therefore you should spread your money across different assets, for example, equities, fixed interest, commercial property and cash. However these investments must be in the right proportions so that they meet your own objectives and attitude to risk. I like to use a lot of alternative investment trusts including things like care homes, student accommodation and renewable energy. These infrastructure trusts have delivered strong returns in recent years although they are more sensitive to political argument and changes which leads to more volatility. And they can be expensive.

Speaker 3: While diversifying your investments, you should also diversify the style of fund manager. Fund managers may have different views on the world and the kind of company likely to perform best; one style or another can come into its own at different points in an economic cycle. For example, some managers invest in high-growth markets such as technology, where stocks can be more expensive but growth is often impressive. In contrast, so-called "value investors" buy very cheap, unloved stocks that they hope will do well during an economic recovery. In recent years, the best funds to own were those linked to high-growth technology companies. But those stocks are expensive, leading to bigger potential losses if results are disappointing.

Speaker 4: Investors should always have a cash safety net to protect them against falling stock markets. Having this cash buffer means they won't be forced to sell when prices are falling. Everybody needs some savings to cover at least three to six months of personal expenditure so they can avoid taking on expensive debt or selling their investments at the wrong time if money is needed at short notice. If you've got a known spending goal in the near term, such as a new car, then cash might be your best option. But if your aim is to retire in a few decades with enough to fund your life then cash is unlikely to deliver that goal.

Speaker 5: Investing is about timing but it's so difficult to predict what markets are doing, that my advice is to drip feed money into the market on a regular basis. This takes the emotion out of investing. It also means the price you pay for stocks and funds will average out over time. With this approach, if investments fall in value, then units are simply bought cheaper next time, bringing down the average purchase cost. Not only does this ensure you don't take too much risk, but by selling investments that have done well in favour of those that have done badly you're effectively selling at the top of the market and buying at the bottom. An investor's ideal goal!

1.2 Intonation in question tags

P1.01

1 Something's wrong here, isn't it?
2 Nobody's joining us, are they?
3 Please call later, will you?
4 Let's get started, shall we?
5 Everyone lives in the area, don't they?
6 Nothing's clear in this report, is it?
7 We rarely ask general questions in surveys, do we?
8 Someone with less time would have more of a problem, wouldn't they?

P1.02

1 Participants should try to agree with each other, shouldn't they?
2 If it wasn't too expensive, you'd go there sometimes, wouldn't you?
3 There isn't anything like this at the moment, is there?
4 It really combines convenience with healthy eating, doesn't it?
5 Participants of focus groups should all be very similar, shouldn't they?
6 That seems to be what we all want, doesn't it?
7 Let's see if we can fix it, shall we?
8 We're all looking forward to the course, aren't we?

1.3 Indian English pronunciation

P1.03

1 outside the scope
2 the main question
3 time to look at
4 about this issue
5 when I talked about
6 to be mindful that
7 the answer to that question
8 Is that OK?

P1.04

1 It's not something we have time to look at today.
2 I'm not entirely sure of the answer to that question.
3 I'll respond directly to you. Is that OK?
4 That question is outside the scope of today's presentation.
5 We need to be mindful that many people feel very strongly about this.
6 We covered that at the beginning of the presentation when I talked about .....
7 What's the main question you have on this?
8 You'd be better off asking my colleague in Finance about this issue.

2.2 Intonation in cleft sentences

P2.01

1 What I'll do tomorrow is to make sure the contract is ready.
2 It was the boring work that made him leave.
3 Something they forgot to take was the latest version of the agreement.
4 What we'll have to rethink are our conditions of employment.
5 It's the supplier in Mexico that my boss is trying to reach.
6 The innovation that didn't work was the one that was most expensive.

P2.02

1 A: Have you managed to get through to the supplier in Mexico yet?
    B: It's my boss that's trying to get through to them.
2 A: Have you managed to get through to the supplier in Mexico yet?
    B: It's the manufacturer in Mexico I'm trying to reach.
3 A: I thought they liked the ideas?
    B: What they criticised was the lack of time to implement them.
4 A: I think he left because of the atmosphere in the office, didn't he?
    B: What made him leave was the boring work he had to do.
5 A: He says he left because of the boring work.
    B: What made me leave was the atmosphere in the office.
6 A: They took various versions of the agreement with them.
    B: Unfortunately the only one they forgot to take was the latest one.

P2.03

1 A: Have you managed to get through to the supplier in Mexico yet?
2 A: Have you managed to get through to the supplier in Mexico yet?
3 A: I thought they liked the ideas?
4 A: I think he left because of the atmosphere in the office, didn't he?
5 A: He says he left because of the boring work.
6 A: They took various versions of the agreement with them.

2.4 Southern U.S. English pronunciation

P2.04

1 from your side
2 you said
3 any quick wins
4 your take on this
5 eye to eye
6 very valid
7 from the agenda
8 increase the insurance

P2.05

1 Do you see any quick wins here?
2 I think both perspectives are very valid.
3 Let me make sure we all understood what you said.
4 Any reflections from your side?
5 We don't really see eye to eye on this.
6 You can see from the agenda what we're all looking to achieve today.
7 We need to increase the insurance for the project.
8 What's your take on this, Jack?

3.2 Stress in phrasal verbs

P3.01

1 She carried on living with her mother.

2 She managed to put some money by each month.
3 She wanted to save up before studying at university.
4 She didn't want to fall behind with the rent.
5 Her grandfather had set up a trust fund for her.

🔊 P3.02
1 He set a trust fund up.
2 He set it up.
3 She wanted to save some money up.
4 The problem has come up before.
5 What if your computer breaks down?
6 He wouldn't be able to pay them back.
7 They agreed to pay off his debts.
8 They agreed to pay them off.

3.3 Chunking and stress in presentations
🔊 P3.03
Then … try and visualise the looks on your guests' faces as they enter the ballroom and see more than one hundred circus performers all dressed in gold. Fire acts! Acrobats! Jugglers! Trapeze artists! All surrounded by enormous golden urns with thousands of flowers cascading from them. Imagine how everyone will react to this incredible sight.

4.2 Weak forms in perfect tenses
🔊 P4.01
1 How many computers had been affected?
2 They still haven't recovered.
3 The ransomware had been aimed at banks.
4 He said he'd been told.
5 They'd chosen their targets carefully.
6 A UK plant will have been targeted.

🔊 P4.02
1 How many computers have been affected?
  How many computers had been affected?
2 They still haven't recovered.
  They still hadn't recovered.
3 The ransomware will be aimed at banks.
  The ransomware had been aimed at banks.
4 He said he's been told.
  He said he'd been told.
5 They'd chosen their targets carefully.
  They've chosen their targets carefully.
6 A UK plant will have been targeted.
  A UK plant will be targeted.

🔊 P4.03
1 Before I worked in this office, I'd never worked at a smart desk.
2 The virus has spread quickly.
3 I've never seen this kind of smart building before.
4 By the time I'd installed it, it was out of date.

5 I've worked for the company for nearly two years.
6 They thought they hadn't been hit, but they had, in fact.
7 They still haven't brought the system back online.
8 They hadn't chosen random targets.
9 I'm sure they'll have been able to respond.
10 I don't think we've been affected, have we?
11 By the end of the day we'll have been given all the details.
12 They thought they'd escaped, but they haven't.

4.4 Volume and tone of voice in challenging conversations
🔊 P4.04
1 A: Experience isn't the only factor we have to take into account.
  B: So, to put it differently, you're saying that my experience didn't matter in this case?
2 A: I agree that you both have similar skills and abilities.
  B: But if I follow you correctly, you mean that he was the better person for the job?
3 A: I'm sorry that we weren't able to give you the team leader position on this occasion.
  B: The fact of the matter is that I'm a little confused and disappointed not to have got the position.
4 A: Of course we've been very impressed by your recent performance.
  B: Yes, can we talk about that for a moment?
5 A: He did a very good job on the last project.
  B: But are you perhaps overlooking the fact that he asked for my assistance at several key points?
6 A: We have a major new project coming up which you could be involved in.
  B: OK, so what exactly would need to happen to move forward from here?

5.1 Stress patterns in word building
🔊 P5.01
culture
process
processed
shipping
assign
assigned
employ
cultural
globalised
immigrant
mobilise

taxable
adopted
assignment
taxation
employee
relocate
secondee
immigration
relocated
compensatory
globalisation

🔊 P5.02
1 accommodation
2 helpful
3 personal

4 development
5 compensation
6 interpreter
7 opportunities
8 permanently
9 organisation

5.2 Stress and intonation in inversions
🔊 P5.03
1 Rarely does anyone I know get any really exciting opportunities.
2 Little did I know how difficult it would be to learn a new language.
3 Never in my life have I been treated so badly by an employer.
4 Not only was the work interesting, but I also got to know something of a different culture.
5 At no time was she offered any kind of support.
6 No sooner had she arrived than she knew she'd be happy there.
7 In no way am I saying that you were responsible for what happened.
8 On no account should you sign the contract in its present form.
9 Only much later did I realise what a great experience it had been.
10 Not only did they have to book a flight, but they also had to find accommodation.
11 Not until he began the job did he realise it was the opportunity of a lifetime.
12 Under no circumstances would I accept that assignment abroad.

6.2 Weak forms in past modals
🔊 P6.01
1 They must have been working late.
2 You oughtn't to have left the company.
3 They couldn't have left on time.
4 You should take the other job.
5 They can't have known that the brand would become so popular.

🔊 P6.02
1 They must be working late.
  They must have been working late.
2 You ought to have left the company.
  You oughtn't to have left the company.
3 They can't have left on time.
  They couldn't have left on time.
4 You should take the other job.
  You should have taken the other job.
5 They couldn't have known that the brand would become so popular.
  They can't have known that the brand would become so popular.

🔊 P6.03
1 Don't you think we should have joined forces?
2 We obviously couldn't have predicted what the results of the merger would be.
3 They could really have kept the brand name, couldn't they?
4 There might have been a lot of different possibilities.

5 They may have wanted to make use of synergy.

6 Shouldn't you have left earlier to be on time for your appointment?

7 The company could actually have grown faster under different ownership.

8 A strategic alliance might perhaps have been a good idea.

9 Couldn't you have taken on the new role you were offered?

10 They can't possibly have told you the details, because they don't know them themselves yet.

11 They must have been trying to decrease competition, mustn't they?

12 They say we should have solved the problem months ago, but I can't see how we could have.

6.4 Scottish English pronunciation

◀) P6.04

1 with hindsight
2 main lesson learnt
3 roles and responsibilities
4 the main problem was
5 proud of what
6 different versions
7 hadn't expected
8 what are your

◀) P6.05

1 Considering everything that happened I'm very proud of what we achieved.

2 In future, roles and responsibilities should be defined more clearly.

3 My main lesson learnt is that problems need to be addressed early.

4 With hindsight, we should have used a project planning tool.

5 One thing I hadn't expected was that they'd need so much guidance.

6 What are your thoughts on this?

7 In many ways, I think that the main problem was a leadership failure.

8 This created the problem that people had different versions of the schedule.

7.1 Linking between words

◀) P7.01

1 two or more floors
2 four earthquakes
3 so always remember
4 Do you always check?
5 more emergencies
6 Is this door a fire door?
7 better equipment
8 for emergency use only

◀) P7.02

1 Keep the weight of the building as light as possible.

2 Many buildings have to be demolished after earthquakes.

3 Buildings in the capital are more at risk than those in other areas.

4 How do earthquakes affect business and the economy?

5 Have you ever worked in a skyscraper?

6 Fire alarms are an effective means of saving lives.

7 Smart systems automatically reduce risk to people in a building.

8 The lifts stop automatically at the nearest floor.

7.2 Intonation in conditionals

◀) P7.03

1 If he were a teenager today, he probably wouldn't have spent his early childhood playing the violin.

2 If he hadn't decided to pursue a graduate degree in economics, he wouldn't have gravitated towards uncertainty.

3 If it hadn't been for a chance meeting, he wouldn't have revolutionised the investment industry.

4 If he hadn't got interested in economics, he might have become a great violinist.

5 If he hadn't struck up a conversation with a stockbroker, we wouldn't be applying his thinking to markets today.

6 If stocks are more volatile than bonds, investors should expect better returns.

7 If he hadn't made a key contribution to economics, he wouldn't have received a Nobel Prize.

8 If he hadn't spent so much time playing baseball, perhaps his interest in economics would have developed earlier.

◀) P7.04

1 a teenager today
   playing the violin
2 a graduate degree in economics
   gravitated towards uncertainty
3 a chance meeting
   revolutionised the investment industry
4 interested in economics
   a great violinist
5 a conversation with a stockbroker
   to markets today
6 more volatile than bonds
   better returns
7 a key contribution to economics
   a Nobel Prize
8 playing baseball
   developed earlier

8.2 South African English pronunciation

◀) P8.01

1 your gut feeling
2 two weeks from now
3 hire someone to help
4 follow your heart
5 the go-ahead
6 all the alternatives
7 type of store
8 a plan of action

◀) P8.02

1 What type of store would you like to open, and where would you want to locate it?

2 The good news is that we've finally got the go-ahead from the CEO.

3 Of course you have to analyse all the different options, but in the end I think it's often best to go with your initial gut feeling.

4 Let's all get together two weeks from now, to evaluate what progress we've made.

5 There isn't much time left, and we urgently need to settle on a plan of action.

6 If you don't hire someone to help you, you'll end up having to do all the work yourself.

7 If you don't think through all the alternatives carefully, you might end up regretting your decision.

8 When you have to make an important decision, do you think it's better to follow your heart or your head?

8.4 Stress and intonation in relationship-oriented decision-making

◀) P8.03

1 There's no easy way to say this, so I'll just say it.

2 Let's put it on hold for a few weeks.

3 How do you think we can get beyond this?

4 Initially, it looked like a good idea, but now I'm not so sure.

5 I don't want to cause any hostility between us.

6 To be honest, I have an issue with the lack of support we have for this.

7 Future collaboration is in both of our interests.

8 How will it negatively affect you?

9 We'd both like to find a quick resolution where we can keep all interests in focus.

10 We both have the same perspective.

11 We need to think about both mutual and individual gain.

12 I'd like to get a feeling for your priorities.